feminine,
free, &
faithful

feminine, free, & faithful

revised and updated

Ronda Chervin

FRANCISCAN UNIVERSITY PRESS
Franciscan University of Steubenville
Steubenville, Ohio

Franciscan University Press
Franciscan University of Steubenville
Steubenville, Ohio 43952
© 1987, 1995 by Ronda Chervin
All rights reserved. First edition 1987
Second edition 1995
Printed in the United States of America

Scripture quotations are from the *Revised Standard Version, Catholic Edition, of the Holy Bible,* © 1965, 1966 by the Division of Christian Education of the National Council of the Churches of Christ in the United States of America.

Cover design: Kinsey Advertising

ISBN 0–940535–83–1

Contents

Preface

Feminine, Free and Faithful was written in 1984 and published in 1986. Since then many developments in the Catholic world—such as the *Apostolic Letter on the Dignity and Vocation of Women* and the magisterium's definitive rejection of proposals for the ordination of women—make an update of the book essential.

Much of the original remains, but with significant changes; many from contributions not only of Catholic women writers, but also of the women who have attended lectures and workshops based on the original *Feminine, Free and Faithful.*

Ronda Chervin

Introduction

I believe that within all women there is a deep desire to be *feminine.* With rare exceptions, women prefer to be considered warm, not cold; charming, not repressed; and wise, not merely critical.

I believe that within all women there is also a deep desire to be *free:* a desire to be daring and spontaneous rather than frightened and stiff; to be strong and initiating, not weak and dependent; to be objective and rational, not unrealistic and irrational.

I believe that being *faithful* to God is the key to unfolding the feminine and free personality. The faithful woman has the strength to use her feminine gifts for the good of the kingdom that Christ came to form "on earth as it is in heaven." The faithful woman has the love that enables her to use her freedom for the good of everyone she encounters.

My experiences have been both the source and the impetus for writing *Feminine, Free, and Faithful.* I am a widow, the mother of three (two young women and one son), and grandmother of four. A professor of philosophy and theology at Franciscan University of Steubenville, I teach courses in the concept of the feminine. A convert to Catholicism, I come from a Jewish, though atheistic, background. I am a writer and speaker, and was one of the five women consultants to the United States Bishops who tried to write a pastoral on the concerns of women. I conduct workshops around the world under the title of *Freed to Love: Healing for Catholic Women.*

As a consultant to the bishops for ten years I daily heard the opinions of Catholic women: they voiced all sides with impulsive cries and polished manifestos. More and more I noticed an "either-or" developing: either women should be feminine and forget about liberation *or* they should be liberated and realize that "femininity" is a euphemism for slavery.

The growing division of Catholic women into these two groups troubles me. Generally those in the "pro-feminine" contingent believe in absolute adherence to the teachings of the Church, but do not recognize any need for liberation; and those who are "pro-liberation" see Church teaching as a hindrance to freedom and seek change.

I have always thought that women could be both feminine and free, and that loving fidelity to the teachings of the Church is not a hindrance to but rather the necessary condition for creative growth. I wrote the first version of this book to *prove* that there was a way to avoid false alternatives.

However, while using my book in courses at catechetical institutes and seminaries and in workshops at retreat houses, I realized that intellectual clarity must be balanced by personal healing in the areas of the feminine and masculine. And so in this, my second edition, I have combined facts and concepts with suggestions for individual appropriation.

Although I wrote *Feminine, Free, and Faithful* primarily for women, I have found that many men also consider it an important book. It can help them understand the teachings of the Church and recognize masculine ambivalence toward women in daily life.

This book shares my experiences of being feminine, free, and faithful, in the hope that this will lead women to consider their own experiences.

Approach of this book

In the first section of the book, devoted to femininity, I explore positive and negative feminine traits. I investigate the roots of these traits from biological, psychological, and sociological viewpoints. I then consider the theory of *complementarity,* maintaining that feminine and masculine traits fit men and women complementarily, which ultimately fosters good relationships.

In the second section, devoted to freedom, I consider the difference between freedom from oppression and freedom to be oneself in the service of God. I demonstrate the compatibility of the elements of freedom—spontaneity, daring, strength, leadership, and objectivity—with femininity and faithfulness. I then analyze feminism and the Jungian theory of wholeness in their positive and negative aspects.

In both sections I address women in the single, married, and consecrated life. Further, I highlight women saints, especially Mary, the Mother of God, as our "foremothers" and heroines; for surely in these women we have tangible proof that being a woman of faith means being both feminine and free.

In the section devoted to faithfulness I present the theological foundations for the Church's teaching on the feminine, including the major consequences it has for ethics, and give suggestions for healing prayer. I evaluate protests concerning language and the roles of women in the Church, and give more suggestions for healing prayer.

Making this study personal

Now that you have a better idea of what you will find in these pages, make this study more personal by answering some key questions. I will give my response; you can answer either mentally or in a notebook. Sharing your responses with another person or in a group can be quite helpful.

—*When have you felt most feminine?* The occasions when I have felt most feminine include: receiving the male sexual explosion of energy, especially when there is hope of new life; experiencing pregnancy; and enjoying the beauty of my children while breast-feeding. I would also include those times when my relentless mind reaches a state of stillness and I can simply enjoy the presence of others, when I can flow with love for family, friends, and God.

—*When has femininity seemed most like a trap?* I feel this way when some traditional feminine duty interferes with my natural inclinations: for example, when I have to clear the table but would prefer to hear what a guest is going to say next, or when I must respond to a child's needs just when I am at a peak in my writing. I also feel angry when my ideas are dismissed because I am a woman and "therefore unimportant." While this is rarer nowadays, it is nonetheless annoying when it does occur.

—*When do you feel most free?* I feel freest when I am spontaneous in a usually formal situation. It gives me enormous joy when, in the middle of a class, I think of something creative to do and immediately put it into practice. I also feel free when someone shows me that I am loved for myself and not for some beneficial role I can play.

—*When does your own freedom feel most dangerous to your welfare or that of others?* I feel terrified when I see that some whimsical stance, born of insecurity, alienates me from others, leaving me in the cold. I am consumed with guilt when I realize that some wild decision of mine could bring about permanent harm to myself or my loved ones.

—*When do you feel most feminine, free, and faithful?* I can be all of these when living out the truths of the Catholic faith. At daily Mass I feel feminine because I am in a yearning, surrendering interior posture. I feel free because I choose to center my soul on God in this manner. I am faithful because I give God the honor that is his due and receive Jesus into my person, as he so desires. I am taken up in awe of my Lord's great gesture of love in sacrificing himself for me and entering my very body each day. I also can be feminine, free, and faithful when I am loving toward my family, especially by openly expressing affection. (Doing chores feels less free.) When lecturing or ministering to a receptive group of Christians I feel most feminine, free, and faithful as the Holy Spirit moves through me so that the doctrines of the Church glow with mystical fire.

—*Who are women you have known or read about who seem to embody femininity, freedom, or faithfulness, or all three?* For feminine warmth I think of my mother, who never let her children go to sleep without a hug and whose bed was an ever-available refuge. For feminine grace I think of my twin sister, a dancer, whose ethereal, beautiful movements enchant me. For freedom I think of unconventional heroines such as Emily Dickinson, Caryll Householander, and Flannery O'Connor. Women who are feminine, free, and faithful include Mary and my favorite saints, who are like spiritual sisters to me: Mary Magdalene, Catherine of Siena, Teresa of Avila, Thérèse of Lisieux, and Elizabeth Ann Seton. Also on my list are modern-day women such as Adrienne von Speyr, Alice von Hildebrand, and Mother Teresa of Calcutta.

While writing *Feminine, Free, and Faithful,* my prayer has been that this book may help me as well as you to develop the best qualities of femininity and freedom as faithful daughters of the Church.

I. Feminine

1
Femininity Defined

On a Saturday morning a group of women in a diner gossip and giggle about other women in parish leadership. They focus on the faults, mannerisms, and ideas—different from their own—of these women.

An observer might remark: "What silly, petty women!"

Suddenly the teenage son of one of the women bursts in with the news that Dad has just been in a serious car accident and is being rushed to the hospital. Mom rushes out the door, face contorted with anguished compassion. The other women hurriedly pay the bill and take the woman's children to their own homes for care and comfort during this emergency.

The observer might now remark: "What wonderful, nurturing women!"

These incidents illustrate traits considered more feminine than masculine: compassion and motherliness; but also gossiping and silliness. There are many traits, positive and negative, that we generally associate with women rather than men. Let us look into some of these.

A. Feminine Traits

While the word *female* refers to the biological characteristics of girls and women, the term *feminine* has a wider reference. *Feminine* pertains to traits associated with the womanly personality (although these traits are also present in another manner in some men). Many people would call certain qualities (some positive, some negative) particularly feminine. Below is a list of some of these qualities. Check the ones you think describe you; circle the ones you wish you were to a greater degree.

Feminine Traits

affectionate	manipulative
capable	modest
catty	moody
charming	nagging
chatter-box	naive
compassionate	nurturing
complaining	obedient
considerate	overly sensitive
delicate	passive
diplomatic	perceptive
empathetic	petty
enduring	polite
expressive	pouty
faithful	prudish
fearful	pure
flirtatious	quiet
gentle	receptive
gossipy	responsive
graceful	seductive
hospitable	sentimental
hysterical	silly
intuitive	sincere

slavish	trusting
smothering	vain
spiritual	vulnerable
spiteful	warm
supportive	weak
sweet	weepy
talkative	wise
tender	wishy-washy

Of the above, most participants in my workshops on the feminine consider the following to be positive descriptions:

affectionate (vs. prudish), charming, compassionate, considerate, delicate, diplomatic, empathetic, enduring, expressive, faithful, gentle, graceful, hospitable, intuitive, modest, nurturing, obedient, perceptive, polite, pure, quiet, receptive, responsive, sincere, spiritual, supportive, sweet, tender, trusting, vulnerable (in the sense of emotionally open), warm, wise

Some well-known women from history, literature, and contemporary life exhibit many of these positive feminine traits: Ruth, Naomi, Sarah; St. Anne, St. Elizabeth, Mary the Mother of God, St. Gertrude, St. Elizabeth of Hungary, St. Thérèse of Lisieux, St. Elizabeth Ann Seton, and many other women saints; Cordelia of *King Lear,* Melanie in *Gone with the Wind;* Grace Kelly and Mother Teresa of Calcutta.

In my unofficial survey, most people consider these to be negative feminine descriptions:

catty, chatter-box, complaining, flirtatious, manipulative, moody, nagging, naive, passive, petty, pouty, prudish, seductive, sentimental, silly, slavish, smothering, spiteful, vain, weak, weepy, wishy-washy

Shakespeare put in the mouth of Iago, the villain of *Othello*, this derisive description of the feminine:

> You are pictures out of door
> Bells in your parlors, wildcats in your
> kitchens,
> Saints in your injuries, devils being
> offended,
> Players in your housewifery, and house-
> wives in your beds.
>
> (*Othello*, II.i.107–110)

Famous women who manifest negative feminine traits include Delilah, Salome, Herodias, Medea, Cleopatra, Ophelia, Margaret of Goethe's *Faust*, Madame Butterfly, Anna Karenina, Grushenka of *The Brothers Karamazov*, Scarlett O'Hara, Elizabeth Taylor, Marilyn Monroe, Blanche of *A Streetcar Named Desire*, Jean Harris, Dolly Parton in her typical film roles, Lucy of "I Love Lucy," Edith Bunker of "All in the Family," Alexis of "Dynasty."

The Nature of Feminine Traits

Positive feminine traits can be grouped into three clusters: warmth, charm, and intuitiveness. Negative feminine traits can be grouped under the negative opposites of these clusters: coldness or smothering, repression or seduction, and over-criticism or subjectivism.

Warmth vs. Coldness

A warm woman exhibits a combination of traits: responsiveness, compassion, empathy, endurance, gentleness, tenderness, hospitality, receptivity, sensitivity, consideration, courtesy, supportiveness, and faithfulness. Such a woman is said to be motherly, loving, or, in modern parlance, nurturing.

Warmth is not only the opposite of coldness but also of the distortion of affection that is found in smothering, which includes negative feminine traits such as pettiness, manipulativeness, complaining, nagging, pouting, and spitefulness.

Warmth is a response of love to the neediness of others. A woman who is empathetic and sensitive is highly aware of the vulnerability of others and reaches out to them.

In the single life, womanly warmth expresses itself in the family, in work situations, in the parish and community, and in friendships with women and men. Married women lavish warmth primarily on their husbands and children. Consecrated religious women manifest warmth largely in prayer, in their communities, and in ministry.

Coldness comes from self-preoccupation: signals that others are in need do not reach the heart. This self-preoccupation usually springs from deep psychological causes, such as inadequate mothering, or from past experiences of feeling victimized by particular types of individuals, so that one may be cold toward one group yet warm toward others.

The need to smother usually results from an insecurity about oneself and others. Afraid of failure, such a woman surrounds others with her worried precautions, nags them to succeed, and feels personally deflated when loved ones show their shortcomings.

Charm vs. Seduction

The word charm originally characterized a word or thing thought to have magic power (the word *charm* comes from the Latin *carmen,* meaning song, from *canere,* to sing). A charming woman is one who attracts and delights.

Charm is a composite of sweetness, grace, expressiveness, delicacy, sensual receptivity, and the emotional openness we call vulnerability.

Some consider charm a synonym for physical beauty; yet we all know women whose physical perfection seems plastic and stiff, and others who are not conventionally attractive yet who emanate charm. It is said that Alma Mahler, wife of Gustav Mahler, was a large, clumsy woman and yet even in her seventies charmed the milkman at her door!

A single woman exudes charm as a daughter and a sister in a family and in school, work, and social life.

While a married woman should be especially charming with her husband and children, she is also charming with relatives, guests, and people at work.

A woman religious becomes charming in her bridal relationship with Christ, as the imagery of the Song of Songs describes. This charm expresses itself in her relationships with others—not as a prelude to sexual intimacy, but as a delicate receptivity and appreciation or a warm unrepressed presence.

It is easy to see what charm is by considering its opposite, a repressed plainness. A locked-up woman is unresponsive, often bitter and resentful; she lacks the delicacy to appreciate what is lovable in others. Many repressed women are shy, which seems to exonerate them from blame. Yet psychologists show that shyness, while rooted in sad childhood circumstances, also demonstrates a self-absorbed fear of being hurt, an unwillingness to risk hurt in order to affirm others.

Charm's negative opposite is called seductiveness. While the genuinely charming woman wants to show her responsiveness to others because she values them, the flirtatious or seductive woman wants the thrill of conquest. The seductress is not concerned with the other person except as one who can confirm her own sexual value (even though she may not even like sex very much). In contrast, the charming, affectionate woman is aware of the attractiveness of others and indicates this by a sort of playfulness of positive warmth.

Intuitiveness vs. Subjectivism

The feminine trait of intuitiveness is somewhat controversial. It doesn't mean having hunches, but coming to a truth through a perceptiveness and a wisdom that is deeper than the analytic process. For example, by philosophical analysis one can demonstrate the need for the existence of God, but most women prefer to *find* God through intuitions of his presence in beauty and goodness.

Intuition is the opposite of overly critical, destructive reasoning. Intuition pierces to the center of reality, whereas the analytic process merely circles and takes jabs at it. But intuition is also the opposite of subjectivity, in which emotion overtakes reason to yield biased or sentimental ideas instead of truth.

Single women might demonstrate intuitiveness in their relationships within the family, at school, at work, in the parish community, and in friendships. Often single women, less burdened by family duties, will become informal or formal counselors, using their intuitive gifts to benefit others.

Married women greatly need intuition in their dealings with husband and children, because they must adapt general truths to their loved ones' individual characters.

Women religious need intuitive wisdom to respond to God revealed in his teachings and providence, lest they lose their faith through the influence of rationalistic trends.

B. Roots of the Feminine

We can gain deeper insights into feminine traits by examining their roots. Various disciplines, such as biology, psychology, and sociology, offer theories about the sources of feminine traits. It is important to cover some of these ideas in detail because Christian feminists, in critiquing magisterial teachings, often assume that natural knowledge does not substantiate Catholic concepts.

Biological Features of the Feminine

Since I am a philosopher and spiritual writer and not a biologist, there's no way I can present a definitive analysis of the research, past and present, concerning the biology of the sexes. Nonetheless, it is important to consider them. We often hear references to the *merely* biological differences between men and women, as if these considerable differences had little relationship to real masculine and feminine characteristics. I agree instead with those thinkers who hold that physical differences are the manifestations as well as the causes of many psychological, intellectual, and spiritual differences.

As you read this section you may want to make it more personal by pausing to consider how a particular fact or theory corresponds to your own thoughts and feelings as a woman.

Here are key points culled from many sources concerning the biological differences between males and females:

— Males have more muscle than females.
— In any given population, the average male height and weight will exceed the female average.
— The human male is more susceptible to many diseases and birth defects.
— Females on the average live longer than males.
— Females mature earlier.
— The female hormonal system operates on a more cyclical pattern.
— Male and female brains differ.
— Males and females differ in sex organs, body hair, and vocal pitch.

Some thinkers hold that greater physical strength naturally leads to dominance and aggressiveness as part of the male role of insuring the physical survival of the tribe. Studies of male primate behavior may indicate this (Tiger and Fox 1971).

According to Darwin, natural selection, the survival of the fittest, determined that men have stronger, bigger bodies and wider, more muscular shoulders than women. Women differ from men just as mares differ from stallions. Man reacts to nature by attack and penetration; he fights animals and conquers forests. He is "against" nature. In contrast, woman is more in tune with nature because of her birthing cycles.

According to Freud, females are passive because they have less libido, or life energy. Women may be considered physically weaker because so much of their biological energy goes into reproductive functions: menstruation, childbearing, and breast-feeding. In addition, man's sexual nature involves the aggressive thrust of the penis with the woman in a submissive posture.

Darwinian and Freudian interpretations of biology, however, need not lead to the assumption that women are biologically inferior or secondary. According to Hans Urs von Balthasar in "Ephesians 5:21–33 and *Humanae Vitae:* A Meditation," in *Christian Married Love* (1981, 62),

> competent biologists have expressed the view that the basic embryonic structure of all living beings, including man, is primarily feminine, and the subsequent differentiation of the male arises from a tendency towards extreme formations, while the development of the female shows a persistence in the original balance.

In an article by Jo Durden-Smith, "Male and Female—Why?" we find this surprising information: "A female fetus has two 'X' chromosomes. . . . The natural form of the human is female. It is the male's 'Y' chromosome that interferes with the natural development by causing production of something called H—Y antigen. This coats the developing gonads . . . and forces them instead to become testicles . . . [that] pump out a hormone which absorbs the female structures that would have become the womb . . . and then they produce testosterone, which . . . causes the progressive reshaping of the male genitalia" (Durden-Smith in *The Collegiate Career Woman,* 1980).

Clearly it is biased thinking to consider the strength to move boulders the model for physical prowess, and the ability to bear children an inferior function. The biological energy required by female functions might instead be considered to make women superior.

Relating this information to negative and positive feminine traits, one might say that relative muscular weakness is a root of the passivity of women in male/female relations. On the other hand, a woman's ability to bear children carries with it advantages for expressing the positive feminine traits of empathy and warmth. What is more, the greater delicacy of the feminine frame has a lot to do with positive traits of charm and evocation of the lyrical. Think of the beauty of the body of the ballerina as the male dancer supports her graceful movements.

Another biological feature that greatly affects feminine traits is the menstrual cycle. Psychiatrist Karl Stern in *The Flight from Woman* (1965) considers it a positive feature of the female to be tied to nature and unable to control it. He points out that "mother" and "matter" are related words and that because of her cycle woman has *time* in her own body in a deeper way than man does.

Women scholars in many fields tend to be interested in the ways the menstrual cycle contributes to the development of negative feminine traits. Differing energy levels throughout the cycle can lead to nervousness and moodiness. A woman is much more responsive in relationships and in work situations at certain times of her cycle than at others. The frequent presence of pain, often severe, during the menstrual flow, certainly causes many a woman to feel victimized by her sexuality, and consequently she may be tempted to nag or lash out at the men in her environment (see Harding 1971).

The female experience of the sex act itself may also affect negative and positive feminine traits.

The woman's sexual organs are basically concave and thus suitable to receive a convex object, the penis. While Karl Stern believes this phenomenon contributes positively to feminine receptivity, Simone de Beauvoir (1952) in *The Second Sex* writes that the female's sexual shape is a symbol of humiliation and slavery. A foreign body can penetrate and enter her. The male's experience of sex involves no such violation of his interiority. The male penis represents his agility and strength, while the woman's concavity represents her inferior immanence. She can only receive by waiting and then clinging, a negative posture, according to de Beauvoir.

I agree with Stern that the woman's sexual role is positive–receptive. In the sex act the woman provides a home for the male, even a symbolic return to the womb. On the other hand, a woman must be open to receive the power of the male's sexual entry.

Self-images of independent completeness and overly ambitious desires for fulfillment on her own terms may block a woman's experience of the joy of receiving the mysterious otherness of a man. Women who are puritanical about sex may be refusing to accept that they have a female body, desiring to remain intact or hating to need others. The body is seen as a dirty, alien, and uncontrollable thing.

Lesbianism may be related in part to a resentment toward this invasion by the dominant male, creating a preference for the equality of the mutual touch in female/female sexual relations. Masturbation, as a sexual lifestyle, could also be viewed in some cases as a bid for autonomy and as a means for avoiding the vulnerability that women feel in male/female sexual relations.

Some psychologists consider the essence of female sexual joy to be related to the desire to be impregnated rather than orgasm, however subjectively pleasurable the latter might be. Karl Stern thinks it is a woman's sexual nature to want to hold and envelop the male organ inside her just as she will eventually envelop the child. He finds the contemporary emphasis on female orgasm to be a masked form of frigidity.

It would seem self-evident that childbearing is the apex of the feminine experience of life. Yet in our society it has become almost peripheral, largely due to a contraceptive mentality. Our urban manner of living permits pregnancy to be almost a private event and militates against the consciousness of pregnancy as central to womanhood. Compare this to the vision a young girl would have of her own future were she living in a small village. There she would know of the birth of babies within a day, watch them being breast-fed, and perhaps every few years count one new baby born to each fertile woman.

Here again we find a physical root of femininity contributing to both positive and negative traits.

Some of the most endearing womanly qualities stem, if not from the direct experience of pregnancy, at least from the potential for nurturing a tiny human in one's own body. Once the shock of finding oneself pregnant wears off and the morning sickness is over, a woman usually feels extremely tender and sweet toward the miniature person in her womb. No bond, psychologists tell us, is as strong as that between a mother and her child. Many women who abort go through intense anguish at the time their baby would have been born had they carried to term

(Stern 1965). The child is a part of the mother, observed the writer Gertrud von Le Fort (1962), and the mother can feel this being "part of" as something blissful. "Loss" of such oneness accounts for the sadness of postpartum depression.

I recall that, in spite of extreme morning sickness due to a twin pregnancy and fear of yet another miscarriage, I was euphoric in my sense of self during that pregnancy. Proud, dreamy, and content, I walked around as if bearing the Savior. Such memories ratify the statement of Karl Stern (1965) in *The Flight from Woman* that the sense of the infinite importance of the individual is rooted in the experience of pregnancy, birth, and nursing. Every birth is a nativity, a cooperation with God's basic act of creation. A woman develops the warmth of her character as she cherishes her unique baby. As Dietrich von Hildebrand wrote in *Man and Woman,* "Children are the love of the couple made visible" (von Hildebrand 1965, cf. 91–93).

During my last pregnancy, in my middle thirties, this joy reached its peak. Since I had already fulfilled my career goals, I was better able to enter into the mysterious meaning of life itself, which transcended all exterior aims.

I wondered if my previous ambitions had made me too masculine to fully enjoy my first experiences of motherhood. Surely the insight into the masculine world afforded me by my career helped me understand Darwin's idea that women had become more tender and less selfish because of their maternal instincts, while men had become less warm since they had to rival other men. Men had learned to find their delight in competition. Do Darwin's ideas also explain why men spend their weekends in front of the TV set watching other men compete at sports?

In "Male and Female—Why?" Durden-Smith provides a sociological perspective:

> For 99% of human history, we've lived as hunter gatherers. The men have been hunters, loners, requiring pronounced visual skills and goal-direction. The women have lived together in groups with children and the old. So it seems to me evolutionarily adaptive that women have acquired different abilities—social, acculturative, nurturant ones that men, by and large, don't have. . . . This implies a sexual stamping, a generic one . . . in the brain . . . in the fetus . . . reinforced and magnified by our cultural institutions. (Durden-Smith 1980, 14)

So far the writers quoted have emphasized the positive feminine traits that result from the uniquely female ability to bear children in the womb. What about the other side? Simone de Beauvoir, in *The Second Sex*, sees pregnancy as a symbolic enslavement and the child as a sort of parasite gnawing away at the mother's strength. For de Beauvoir the maternal instinct should not be glorified, for it is a mixture of many emotions. Perhaps the experience of being a victim of one's own body can partially explain such negative traits as being self-pitying, weepy, complaining, nagging, and spiteful. This behavior may also be a woman's way of getting even with the impregnating male, who is physically free from the burden of his fertility.

Let's return to the positive experience of the female body and its potentialities. The word "bonding" is being used to describe the link that forms between mother and child during pregnancy and that continues after birth. Many women believe that breast-feeding is part of this bonding process. The hormones that a mother builds up during pregnancy prepare her for breast-feeding and other maternal responses, as indicated in many studies. Breast-feeding, however, has not always been popular in our society. In the beginning of the industrial era, when it became profitable to hire women for factory work, breast-feeding went out of style and the invention of the bottle was considered a wonderful advance. In our day breast-feeding is on the upswing. Studies show that human milk is healthier for the baby than substitutes. The sensual, emotional, and spiritual joys a mother experiences by breast-feeding, as well as the great importance of the bond that nursing creates between the baby and the mother, are being emphasized.

Such physical aspects of mothering affect the development of positive feminine traits. A study of female rats showed an interesting difference in behavior pre- and post-partum: before giving birth, the rat preferred looking for food rather than staying with baby rats in the environment; after giving birth to her own babies, she would remain close to the babies rather than seek food. This could be seen as analogous to the willingness of human mothers to sacrifice for their children.

Some women find that their breasts ache when they imagine their infants are in trouble. Some proponents of breast-feeding, including members of La Leche League, hold that mothers have more empathy for the children they breast-fed than for those they fed with a bottle. One African word for mother means "she who hears when I call."

The physical roots of feminine traits are not limited to women who actually bear children in the womb. Women who adopt can be just as maternal as "birth" mothers, and so can single and celibate women. One explanation, which concurs with the theories of Karl Stern and others, is that biological capabilities affect the whole psychology of a woman whether or not these capabilities are fulfilled.

Another reason all women can be maternal might be that the feminine figure is generally rounder and softer than the male figure. Clothing that emphasizes a woman's breasts has a maternal, earthy appeal as well as a sexual one. To be held by a woman gives one a feeling of sinking into *warmth*, of coming to refuge; being hugged by most men gives one a greater feeling of protective *strength*.

Of course, the same feminine figure can symbolize such negative feminine traits as smothering or promiscuous seductiveness, and such positive traits as beauty and delicacy. Many women are too close to their own bodies, or too intimidated by "perfect" fold-out images, to realize that men find the feminine body in itself attractive.

A woman's genital sexual sphere is veiled and hidden, unlike a man's; this contributes to the mysterious quality men find in women, claims Gertrud von Le Fort (1962) in *The Eternal Woman*. Such factors may heighten the sensual receptivity of women or lead to polar negative traits, a puritanical closedness at one extreme and coquettish attempts to trap a man at the other.

What about brain differences between female and male and their effect on feminine traits such as silliness, being scatterbrained, petty, sensitive, or intuitive? "Male and Female—Why?" summarizes studies on the nature of the brain and its hemi-spheres. These studies indicate that the left hemisphere of the brain, which specializes in visual tasks, mathematics, the perception of spatial rela-tions, and conceptualization, is more developed in most males than in the females. The more developed right brain of females makes them better at verbal skills and more sensitive to nuances. "Females are sensi-tive to context, good at picking up information that is incidental to a task that's set them, and distract-ible" (Durden-Smith 1980, 11–13). This makes them adept at reading emotions in faces and hearing nuances in voices. Such sensitivity can explain why women have so many observations to share when chatting. The appearance of silliness can belie the deeply-rooted need to understand what is going on in personal situations.

While reading a Jane Austen novel, consisting mainly of conversations between women in a small English village, I was struck by this comparison: all the intellectual energy a contemporary woman de-votes to her career used to be expended in arranging daily life situations to insure the greatest comfort and pleasure. In the past a woman worked to create a comfortable environment for her guests; even the character defects of her guests were mitigated by such strategies as well-planned seating arrange-ments or a subtle compliment. One wonders whether our contemporary need to get "high" as quickly as possible on social occasions is related to the lack of interest women now take in studying the intricacies of social interaction. Naturally the same intuitive wisdom once employed for the comfort of others can be used to further selfish purposes as well—for in-stance, in "making contacts" with useful people.

It is often said that women are more intuitive because they combine heart and head more often than their male counterparts do, an idea which can be evaluated negatively or positively. For example, according to Karl Stern, the Spanish philosopher Ortega y Gasset thinks women are less rational and practical than men. Stern describes men as going around objects from the outside in an overly analytic manner, whereas women internalize, permitting reality to enter themselves and coming into intellectual sympathy with an object before drawing conclusions (Stern 1965, 25–26).

Sociological and Psychological Factors

Many battles are being fought between those who believe that negative feminine traits are caused solely by sociological and psychological reinforcement, largely in the interests of men, and those who consider such feminine traits innate. In another, less vitriolic camp, we find those who argue that positive feminine traits are indeed largely dependent upon reinforcement and that the growing lack of such support in our feminist climate is leading to the disappearance of some of the noblest qualities of the human race. Let us examine some very prevalent feminine traits to determine their roots.

Nurturing

Much discussion concerns the concept of nurturing. Woman is seen as one who nurtures, one who provides what is nourishing in the way of food and psychological support. In the past this quality was more simply designated by the words "motherly," "maternal," or, even more simply, "love." Thus Dante wrote that woman possesses the spirit of love. Lord Byron penned these fascinating lines in the poem *Don Juan:* "Man's love is of man's life a thing apart, 'Tis woman's whole existence. . ." (Canto the First, CXCIV).

A child learns to communicate inter-subjectively as he lies in his mother's arms receiving essential food and tenderness. A mother's experience of loving empathy with her needy, completely dependent child may lead her to view all human beings as children who still need her food, her warmth, her compassion. And thus she becomes not only tender but also sensitive. This is why women ought to become nurses, teachers, social workers, and even businesswomen, because they may bring their womanly love into such public situations.

Edith Stein attributes the ability to sense the value of the unique individual to the physical realities of motherhood, where the woman offers her body as home for the precious child (Stein 1987). I would add that in this era, when abortion is available, legal, and socially accepted, childbirth is no longer seen as the inevitable result of sexual intercourse. The choice for motherhood, therefore, requires more conscious attention to the special value of the child.

In a Different Voice by Carol Gilligan (1982) introduces an illuminating idea: Girls become more empathetic because their mothers identify with them as females, whereas boys seem different to the mother. Simone de Beauvoir claims in *The Second Sex* that because women in the past did not compete with men at work, they ratified rather than rivaled the men in their lives. A woman gives a man a kind of rebirth through her faith in him.

The nurturing function of woman can also be related to her special manner of using her mind.

Housewifery, according to Simone de Beauvoir, means giving attention to little things in a limited sphere. While de Beauvoir insists that such a life is an intolerable restriction, G. K. Chesterton, in *What's Wrong with the World?* (1942, 153ff.), argues that work in the home is gloriously universal and superior to the specialized tasks of masculine work in the world. The wife and mother is simultaneously sage, psychologist, doctor, cook, manager, teacher, and so forth. Writing at the dawn of English feminism, he found it contradictory that women wanted to rush out of their homes to do for strangers what they could do more successfully for their own dear families. He quipped that in his time thousands of women shouted, "We will not be dictated to anymore!" then rushed out with their steno pads to take dictation.

An idea of Karl Stern, which I have substantiated by observation, concerns the motives of a woman's thinking process. When men express their ideas, they concentrate on concepts, moving from concept to concrete examples and then returning to the concept. A woman is concerned about the listener's needs; she hunts for a truth that will be relevant to her listener and explains her thoughts in terms of that truth. It would be interesting to study women teachers to test my assumption that they frequently use personal examples, not only for the sake of clarity, but also to make ideas directly significant to the lives of their pupils.

In a novel about women intellectuals (*Gaudy Night*, 1936), Dorothy Sayers explores the idea that although women can be just as brilliant artists or thinkers as men can, few women believe that such creativity is equal to the creativity of love and motherhood.

The concept that women are nurturers is not amorphous. It permeates our culture in vivid images of feminine heroines. I find a strong contrast, for example, between the characters Melanie and Scarlett in the movie *Gone with the Wind.* Scarlett, in selfish pursuit of her own goals, tramples on the needs of those to whom she should be most sensitive. Melanie is her foil, representing all the sweet goodness of positive femininity.

The great Russian novel *Anna Karenina* also depicts a nurturing woman, Kitty, whose virtues are highlighted by the portrayal of an opposite type of woman, Anna. Anna's desire for personal romantic fulfillment leads her to abandon not only her undeserving negative masculine husband but also her beloved son. Obsessed by jealousy of her lover, she can get little joy from the birth of their "love child" and refuses to attempt to conceive the son her lover longs for. Kitty, who chose real love after being rejected in her infatuation-love, enjoys the contentment of motherhood. Anna, who plunged into the world of Eros and desperately sought life, ends in suicide, the total negation of life.

Mary, the Mother of God and the archetypal woman, enters our culture not only spiritually but also visually through millions of paintings and statues. She is depicted as full of compassion and tenderness for the infant Jesus and for us, her spiritual children.

Many of the active women saints are women of universal love, who reach out to help the poor and needy and long to comfort them with their own hands, their own tenderness.

In my childhood on Mother's Day it was traditional to hear a sugary song on the radio called "Mother," in which each letter of the word stood for some maternal virtue. Magazine and TV advertisements induced people to buy their food products by showing a warm, round, motherly type of woman preparing or serving the product.

On the opposite side, women who lacked nurturing qualities have always been excoriated in fairy tales, literature, and the movies. The evil stepmother of Hansel and Gretel, the wicked queen in Snow White, the cruel stepmother of Cinderella—these women must come to a bad end. So, too, must cold, self-absorbed women like Ibsen's Hedda Gabler. Films in the forties and fifties opened with plucky, aggressive women who, by the end of the movie, had been conquered and "feminized" by persistent men.

Most women accepted such images, not because they were weak and silly, but because some deep, earthy wisdom told them that the nurturing qualities of women were essential, and there could be no substitute for them.

In case you are getting nervous at this point, let me remind you that my title includes feminine *and* free. By the end of the book I hope to have shown that a woman's strength, vitality, and sense of adventure need not be sacrificed for her to be feminine—indeed, they can be part of it.

Let us turn now to the distortions of nurturing outlined earlier: nagging, possessiveness, and smothering.

In New York City I once witnessed a scene that has helped me to understand how these distortions come about. A tiny, filthy playground among the tall buildings had no heavy rubber safety pads under the equipment. Tiny tots would climb up a huge slide and, if their mothers didn't catch them at the bottom, would land with a thud on the concrete. I shall never forget the touching sight of toddlers gleefully screeching their way down the slide, while their mamas stood tensely, arms outstretched, faces taut, waiting to protect them from brain concussions.

This scene became a prime example to me of what philosophers call "contingency." We are finite, fragile human beings; the slightest accident can kill us instantly. We are contingent beings, not an absolute being like God, who remains solidly perfect no matter what happens. The fact of contingency poses a difficult and sometimes unbearable problem for those who love others. When we so keenly appreciate the preciousness of another individual—a child, a husband, a parent, a friend—how can we not become worried, even paralyzed with fear, at the thought of all the dangers that threaten the beloved?

The child sees the world as a wonderful place of possibility, while the mother may come to view it as pure danger. Nagging can be analyzed as a petty way of trying to insure that things go well for loved ones. "Brush your teeth," "comb your hair," "put on your rubbers," etc. All these orders are given to help prevent future suffering such as rotting teeth, social ostracism, or a cold. Though not as extreme as possessiveness and smothering, nagging or henpecking can become extremely disagreeable to the victim. It is inimical to a free, fun-loving atmosphere.

In possessive smothering, the woman wraps herself like a cocoon around her loved ones. First she holds them safe against the frightening world. Then

she tries to mold them into the image that she cherishes for them. Finally, her need to control replaces
any respect for their own individuality and freedom.

In a perceptive passage, the philosopher Edith
Stein describes the negative traits of some women
as "an excessive interest in others . . . curiosity,
gossip, and an indiscreet need to penetrate into the
intimate life of others. . . . [She] *cannot endure quiet,
reserved growth*" (Stein 1987, 45, italics added).
These traits can result in a woman treating others
as if they belonged to her—as her own *things.*

A woman might overcome such possessiveness
by adopting a philosophical attitude, shrugging her
shoulders and uttering a cliché phrase: "So what
can I do about it?" or "What's the use of worrying?"
Personally, I find that only a profound faith in God
permits me to accept the myriad possibilities of suffering that threaten those I love. Only by putting
them into God's hands can I release them from my
own.

A brilliant young student of mine, afflicted with
a smothering mother, phrased it this way: "Bitchi-
ness is fear screaming—this incinerates a man."

Simone de Beauvoir describes the woman who
over-mothers this way: "Her dream is contradictory:
she would have [her son] of unlimited power, yet
held in the palm of her hand, dominating the world,
yet on his knees before her" (de Beauvoir 1952, 487–
88). She keeps him homebound so that she can
control him but also hates him for not being a cham-
pion. Such a paradox can be described in this way:
a woman tries to put the boy or man back into her
womb for fear he will transcend her, tries to close
the gap by keeping him in.

M. Esther Harding (1971) devotes a fascinating, if troubling, chapter of her book *Woman's Mysteries* to "The Sacrifice of the Son." It is socially acceptable to a point, but psychologically dangerous, when a mother sacrifices all her own interests in total devotion to her child. When she behaves in this way, she overprotects the son, who later becomes unable to meet the harsh realities of the world. The son gains the power to become strong only when she pushes him out into the world.

I recall, with tender pride, an early episode in my relationship with my son. Full of admiration for the Montessori method of schooling young children, I sent my boy a little prematurely to such a nursery. I didn't realize that in this particular institution the smallest children would mingle with sixth graders in the playground during the long, undersupervised recesses. During his first week of nursery school, my two-and-a-half-year-old child was clearly terrified of making his way among the ten-year-old giants. But the teacher told me not to worry, he would get used to it sooner or later. So, the third day, I drove him to the school and stood behind the wire fence. My heart breaking, I watched him slowly try to steer a path through the big boys to the safety of his teacher, who was across the yard. About three feet away he turned around and yelled to me, "Mommy, go away! Can't you see I can never do it with you standing there?"

The poet Audre Lorde wrote in a similar vein "boys whisper to their mothers 'Let us sleep in your bed' . . . but she closes the door. They become men" (Lorde 1978, 8).

These references to the psychological and sociological factors of nurturing strengthened me as a mother and helped me understand how the idea of nurturing has been distorted. Similar considerations can be made about feminine charm.

Charm

Years ago teenage girls used to be sent to "charm school" in the hope that they would be transformed from gangling adolescents into suave young ladies. The very idea would make knowing adults smile: charm is a quality much too elusive to be taught. Of course, the graduates of charm school knew how to dress well, how to sit in company with demurely crossed ankles rather than sprawled out on a sofa, how to apply makeup discreetly but effectively, and so forth. But is this really the same as being charming? In the popular film *Gigi* a charming but ill-bred girl is tutored in sophistication in preparation to be mistress to a rich man-about-town. The results horrify him.

Even when we analyze charm and identify its components—sweetness, expressiveness, receptivity, and sensual openness—it remains somewhat elusive. Some women have all these qualities, yet somehow lack a certain piquant element that turns a pleasant, comfortable woman into a charming, feminine one.

Charm in women may well reflect how a father relates to his daughter. Psychologists recognize a certain stage of coquettishness in little girls. A father, brother, or other male figure can respond to such flirtatiousness with delight or sometimes, afraid of responding with too much sensuality, with rejection or disgust. A mother may model charm for her daughter; although sometimes the more attractive a mother, the more inferior a daughter will feel, particularly if she is physically less beautiful. On the other hand, a puritanical mother may punish her daughter for being charming, label her as a manipulator of men, or openly reject her as a potentially "bad" girl.

A negative response to wild, free, girlish traits can stifle natural charm (which I believe is innate in all people), producing stiff, prudish, repressed, and shy daughters. Quietness, when not caused by fear of rejection, can of course be a lovely ingredient in a charming woman.

The charming celibate woman is not prudish; rather she is wide open to the mystical love of God, which encompasses body as well as spirit. The puritanical virgin hates the body and cannot bear the idea of another person entering her. Authentic virginal purity can be a strong positive ingredient in feminine loveliness as well as a Christian virtue.

Simone de Beauvoir claims that a man is attracted to a virgin because he thinks that if no one has used her she can belong to him completely. More cynically, Bertrand Russell in *Marriage and Morals* (excerpted in Mahowald 1978) predicted that without sociological reinforcement of purity, men would refuse to acknowledge as their own the children they had conceived with women who had many lovers. Hence the state would become the father of the children of the future!

A charming but pure woman can use the force of the erotic in the service of genuine love. She can learn how to bring delight into the lives of those around her without luring others into an ultimately unfulfilling intimacy.

Naturally charm in all its facets plays a large role in relationships that have the promise of commitment. Some Christian writers, eager to keep young people from sin, exalt an ideal of brotherly and sisterly affection even for engaged couples. This, I believe, goes too far. Sometimes it merely postpones romantic intimacy to marriage, but it can lead to a lack of openness to intimacy later in the marriage because partners have come to view one another only in practical or purely spiritual terms. In other instances it results in romantic relationships with partners other than the too-brotherly husband. A certain light flirtatiousness in courtship can be positive, though it can become negative if expressed promiscuously.

Sweetness, an aspect of feminine charm at one time revered, is now in danger of extinction. A charming woman, even if she is a free spirit with plenty of passion, is, at the same time, sweet. A more peaceful, contented woman may be "pink lacy" sweet, but there are red-hot ways of being sweet as well. Ice cream is sweet, but so is liqueur.

Sweetness can manifest itself in many different ways. It can be an expression of innocence, a feeling of surrender, or a quality of compassion. Sweetness comes when its opposite, bitterness, either has never been allowed to develop or has been overcome.

The lack of sweetness can signify an unwillingness to be close to others, a desire to be barricaded behind a wall, a tendency to be hard and self-enclosed. Lack of sweetness can also come from immersion in practical tasks and a failure to develop the subtle nuances of love. The sarcastic woman directs her attention to everything ridiculous and defective in others. In contrast, the sweet woman sees the vulnerability behind the bad, and seeks to bring out the better side of others through her faith in them. Nietzsche's dictum, though itself somewhat sarcastic, pronounces a truth: "Woman learns how to hate in proportion as she forgets how to charm."

Such are some of the positive aspects of the feminine virtue of charm. But the word "charm" itself has an ambiguous flavor, conjuring images of magic charms and, with them, a feeling of danger.

In Chinese thought, the feminine "Yin" is dark, shady, stealthy, destructive, and catlike. Love is full of the power to destroy, wrote Sappho, the Greek poetess of the seventh century B.C. Men are afraid of falling under the power of woman as in the famous biblical story of Samson and Delilah or in Shakespeare's *Antony and Cleopatra.*

The seductress uses her sensual openness, her apparent sweetness and empathy, to control men for her own ends. She recognizes in herself and in the man the irrational weakness that sensual love creates: "Love, the limb-loosener, the bitter-sweet torment, the wild beast there is no withstanding" (Sappho).

Gertrud von Le Fort, in *The Eternal Woman* (1962), insightfully notes that while the whore serves the male as his object, she triumphs over him as she watches him become prey to the dark forces of life. In seduction, according to de Beauvoir, the woman drags the man out of his transcendent world of meaningful goals into her own irrational immanence. I wonder what a prostitute might say about such a sophisticated theory.

To focus on less extreme corruptions of charm, we might view the coy, flattering woman as one who wants to please too much. Lacking a sense of her own strengths, she becomes gushy and sentimental in her desire to find good in others on whom she might rely.

The eighteenth-century philosopher Mary Wollstonecraft pointed out in *A Vindication of the Rights of Women* (excerpted in Mahowald 1978) that if a woman cultivates only her charms and not her mind and spirit, she has no inner faculties to rely on in marriage, once the first period of delight is over. When a husband is bored with her superficial traits, she becomes coquettish with other men or vainly obsessed with her looks and clothing.

Wollstonecraft's point is relevant to the image of woman presented in contemporary advertisements. The more shrunken the mind and spirit of a woman, the more she must add to her mask of physical perfection. Behind such foolishness lies a desperate plea—"Love me because I am so charming, so perfectly beautiful"—because she has no hope of being loved for more substantial qualities. Such a woman spends hours before the mirror working on her looks. Narcissism becomes a substitute for the missing self-love that would produce true feminine charm.

Sometimes a woman who devotes no time at all to her personal vanity puts enormous energy into creating a "charming home." Paradoxically, if her only aim is to present an image of perfection, people will not want to visit and her family will be miserable; it is only when a home's decoration is permeated with love, beauty, and a concern for the needs of the inhabitants that a house becomes a place people want to visit and live in.

Once again we see that love makes the differ-ence between the negative and positive ways of being truly feminine, in this case charming. Love is the key to positive femininity.

2
Male/Female Complementarity

Philosophy rarely considers the feminine without also considering the masculine. Throughout history and across cultures many philosophers have pronounced some form of complementarity. Generally they agree that there are *intrinsic* physical, emotional, and intellectual differences between men and women and that these differences make men and women complementary pairs.

Here are some of the complementary qualities of the masculine and feminine that philosophers have distinguished:

Masculine	Feminine
objective	intuitive
analytic	wise
leader	follower
interest in wider world	domestic
task oriented	quality-of-life oriented
light	dark
good	evil
providing	nurturing
hard	soft, delicate
dominating, governing	subservient
brutal	sweet
strong of body and will	weak of body and will
head dominates	heart dominates

creating outside of self	creating within the womb
spiritually active	spiritually contemplative
future oriented	present oriented
sublime	beautiful
adult	childlike

Some philosophers think of men and women as different but equal in their fundamental dignity. These include Augustine, Thomas Aquinas, Rousseau, Kant, C. S. Lewis, the von Hildebrands, Edith Stein, Karl Stern, Karol Wojtyla, and C. G. Allen.

Other philosophers say the differences between men and women indicate the basic inferiority of women. These include Pythagorean thinkers, Aristotle, Schopenhauer, Nietzsche, and Sartre (in part).

Philosophers who emphasize the similarity between men and women are mentioned in the section "Free."

In my research on philosophers' views about the feminine and masculine, I have primarily used two sources: Mahowald's *Philosophy of Woman* (1978), which includes excerpts of many works, and *The Great Books* (Index). Some excerpts do indicate extreme ideas about the "inferiority" of women. However, in some cases, to label a philosopher anti-woman on the basis of particular quotations can be misleading.

A distinction should also be made between *complementarity of qualities* and *complementarity of roles.* Quality-complementarians such as Dietrich von Hildebrand, Stern, and Wojtyla (John Paul II) are primarily concerned that different traits of men and women be reinforced, whatever roles they play in life. Of course, roles of motherhood and fatherhood involve different qualities, but one does not find in quality-complementarity the same emphasis on men and women having opposite positions and tasks in society.

Here are a few theories typical of a quality-complementarian.

Edith Stein, a German phenomenologist who became a Carmelite nun, writes the following:

> I am convinced that the species *human-ity* embraces the double species *man* and *woman;* that the essence of the complete *human* being is characterized by this dual-ity; and that the entire structure of the essence demonstrates the specific character. There is a difference, not only in body struc-ture and in particular physiological functions, but also in the entire corporeal life. The rela-tionship of the soul and body is different in man and woman. . . . The feminine species expresses a unity and wholeness of the total psychosomatic personality and a harmonious development of faculties. The masculine spe-cies strives to enhance individual abilities in order that they may attain their highest achievements. . . .
>
> [Woman's] strength lies in her intuitive grasp of the concrete and the living, especially of the personal. She has the gift of adapting herself to the inner life of others. (Stein 1987, 177, 178)

This gift is related intricately to woman's ability to carry a child within her womb and to breast-feed. Whether she is biologically a mother or not, her whole psyche is geared toward holding others close.

The philosophy of Dietrich von Hildebrand, as summarized in *Man and Woman,* puts forth a specifically quality-complementarian theory with little concern about implications for role-complementarity. This may be partly explained by the fact that von Hildebrand was himself the youngest in a family of remarkably creative and intelligent women. He surrounded himself with similar women throughout his life—his second wife, Alice von Hildebrand, being a philosopher and co-author of several of his books.

Von Hildebrand thinks that men and women are equal in nature and in their call to holiness, yet they are two different *expressions* of human nature.

> The difference in the personality structure of man and woman remains an undeniable reality. If we try to delineate these specifically feminine and masculine features, we find in women a unity of personality by the fact that heart, intellect and temperament are much more interwoven; whereas in man there is a specific capacity to emancipate himself with his intellect from the affective sphere. (Dietrich von Hildebrand 1965, 13)

He points out that the united personality of a woman makes isolated (promiscuous) sexual experiences more destructive for her than for a man. The man committing the same sins is equally culpable, but less annihilated, since he can more readily make sex simply a compartment of his life. In woman the *personality* is more in the foreground; in man, his *activities*.

According to Dietrich von Hildebrand, because men and women are complementary, they are spiritually ordered to each other and created for each other. Greater love is possible between them than between members of the same sex. More fruitfulness is possible because of a certain tension between them, because of their delight in one another. They are more suited to meet in an "I-thou" communion than two of the same sex who join together to appreciate a reality outside themselves.

Perceptively, von Hildebrand saw that the positive masculine liberates woman from the negative feminine and that the positive feminine helps to bring men out of the negative masculine. Men become less coarse, dried out, and depersonalized when women are present and women become less petty, self-centered, and hypersensitive in the presence of men. A man with a strong mind can lift a woman out of the complacency she may fall into. A woman brings out a man's tenderness and responsibility.

Quality-complementarity with a modified role-complementarity is commanding attention from another source: the philosophical and papal writings of John Paul II. "In the sphere of what is 'human'—of what is humanly personal—*'masculinity' and 'femininity' are distinct*, yet at the same time they *complete and explain each other*" (*Mulieris Dignitatem*, n. 25).

In his beautiful book *Love and Responsibility* (written before he became pope), he underscores the equal ontological dignity of women and men. "A woman is capable of truly making a gift of herself only if she fully believes in the value of her person and in the value as a person of the man to whom she gives herself. And a man is capable of fully accepting a woman's gift of herself only if he is fully conscious of the magnitude of the gift—which he cannot be unless he affirms the value of her person" (Wojtyla 1981, 129). And in *Mulieris Dignitatem* he reaffirms this equal ontological dignity: *"Both man and woman are human beings to an equal degree, both are created in God's image. . . . Man is a person, man and woman equally so"* (n. 6).

At the same time, he frequently alludes to complementary differences in feminine and masculine traits similar to the ones we have outlined earlier in this chapter (see Wojtyla [1981] 110, 117, 125 ff., 176 ff., 189).

A playwright as well as a philosopher-theologian, John Paul II frequently captures in a phrase his perception of complementarity, as in: "A woman wants to be loved so that she can show love; a man wants to love so that he can be loved." Or, "Above all the woman . . . feels that her role in marriage is to give herself; the man's experience of marriage is different, since, 'giving oneself' has as its psychological correlative 'possession'" (Wojtyla 1981, 99).

Like Dietrich von Hildebrand, Pope John Paul II sees the "I-thou" communion of man and woman:

> Man cannot exist "alone" (cf. Gen 2:18); he can exist only as a "unity of the two," and therefore *in relation to another human person.* It is a question here of a mutual relationship: man to woman and woman to man. Being a person in the image and likeness of God thus also involves existing in a relationship, in relation to the other "I." . . .
>
> Man and woman, created as a "unity of the two" in their common humanity, are called to live in a communion of love, and in this way to mirror in the world the communion of

love that is in God, through which the Three Persons love each other in the intimate mystery of the one divine life. (*Mulieris Dignitatem*, n. 7)

Familiaris Consortio, Pope John Paul II's "Apostolic Exhortation on the Family" (1981), crystallizes his ideas about men and women in the married state. The passage most often quoted states that wives and mothers must not be *compelled* to work outside the home. In his encyclical on work, *Laborem Exercens*, the Pope suggests a revolutionary plan that would have societies provide women with supplementary incomes so that they might comfortably remain in the home to tend their children without economic pressure to work outside the house.

Pope John Paul II's ideas are primarily quality-complementarian. Expressions of role-complementarity can be found to varying extents in the works of such philosophers as Aristotle, Augustine, Thomas Aquinas, Rousseau, Kant, and Nietzsche. They believe that strong role differentiation, especially concerning males in leadership, furthers the stability and happiness of mankind.

Among the most striking and popular recommendations of role-complementarity are best-selling books such as Marabel Morgan's *The Total Woman* (1975) or Helen Andelin's *Fascinating Womanhood* (1990). These books differ from the sober rendition of scholars and philosophers not only in their rollicking "how to" style, but also in their emphasis on the negative feminine traits. According to these women authors, the more dependent, manipulative, weak, coy, and kittenish the woman, the more she will draw out the positive masculine traits in her spouse.

The happy "success stories" that fill such books raise certain questions about how apt the label "negative" might be in our list of feminine traits. Can it be that some of these qualities, while toxic to society in general, can become positive within the marital union?

Deborah Grumbine—wife, mother of five, and Catholic writer—thinks so. In "How to Be Happy and Holy in Your Own Home," she writes about joy in sex and contentment in family relations, and she depicts a certain merry coyness and frank desirousness as the rewards a tired husband and wife deserve after a hard day of work. Grumbine also believes strongly in the subordination of wives to their husbands. This submissiveness is not passivity, however, for the wife should battle vehemently for her convictions. However, when the husband and wife disagree, the husband has to break the tie not only to avoid chaos or divorce, but also to realize his responsible, forceful leadership qualities. A man in this position will rejoice to know that his decisions have brought happiness to his wife and children. Grumbine's (unpublished) manuscript includes invaluable practical suggestions about happiness in marriage and family.

Truths and Falsehoods of the Complementarity Theory

It is my conviction that quality-complementarity contains precious truths and that role-complementarity, while sometimes too rigid, is basically helpful to women and men. The feminist critique of these theories will be evaluated in chapter four, "Feminism."

Basically I find that women who concentrate on developing masculine traits and on fulfilling masculine roles seem incomplete and unhappy. Women who develop their femininity yet also develop the traditionally masculine traits (such as those listed at the beginning of this chapter) seem more fulfilled.

We are called to exemplify all the virtues, not just the feminine ones. Sometimes romanticism of the feminine or a strict definition of roles can lead to the sort of clinging violet, passive, lovable, but weak woman, such as Edith Bunker of "All in the Family."

Some Catholic women exhibit this deformation by staying in canonically invalid marriages or by continuing in a situation where they are physically or psychologically battered; they do not stay out of love but because they fear independence and the resulting struggle to earn a living. A less drastic form of inadequate development of traditionally more masculine traits occurs when a woman is too shy to witness to her faith.

Men who overemphasize their male-leadership traits without developing Christian maturity can become, at worst, tyrannical and brutal, and, at best, patronizing, paternalistic, and smug.

I have found it stimulating to consider an analysis of the feminine from the standpoint of natural knowledge and wisdom. However, for me this is but a prelude to the enjoyment of the truth to be found through pondering God's will for women in Scripture and Tradition—the feminine transfigured in Christ.

II. Free

3

Freedom Defined

A woman also wants to be free.

Of course the word freedom is ambiguous. For most women, to be free means not to feel trapped, hemmed in; not forced to be someone she is not so as to conform to someone else's idea of what a woman should be. In the Christian sense, freedom is liberation from sin which enables one to love more fully.

This chapter focuses on key traits of freedom: spontaneity and daring versus repression or folly; strength to lead versus passivity or domineeringness; objectivity versus subjectivity or cold analysis. These positive traits of freedom, we will see, support a woman's femininity.

In subsequent chapters of this section, we will investigate the roots of freedom and consider two methods offered in our times for gaining greater freedom for women: feminism and Jungian wholeness.

Traits of Freedom

Listed here are some words that people associate with freedom. Check the ones you think describe you; circle the ones you wish described you.

adventuresome   brave
ambitious   cold
assertive   competitive
authoritative   daredevilish

daring	lustful
decisive	objective
domineering	proud
driving	ruthless
firm	self-controlled
forceful	spontaneous
initiating	strong
just	stubborn
leading	tough
logical	valiant
loud	

Generally people consider the following to be positive descriptors of free women:

adventuresome, assertive, authoritative, brave, daring, decisive, driving, firm, forceful, initiating, just, leading, logical, objective, self-controlled, spontaneous, strong, tough, valiant

Famous women who have exhibited some of these traits include Esther, Deborah, Judith, St. Catherine of Siena, St. Teresa of Avila, St. Joan of Arc, Harriet Tubman, Amelia Earhart, Eleanor Roosevelt, Rose Kennedy, Golda Meir. You can probably add many more.

The following are negative descriptors of free women:

ambitious, cold, competitive, daredevilish, domineering, loud, lustful, proud, ruthless, stubborn

Examples of women who have exhibited some of these negative traits include Herodias, who ordered the beheading of John the Baptist; Livia, the scheming Roman dowager of the time of the Caesars; Lady Macbeth; and Lucretia Borgia.

The Nature of Freedom

Freedom can be defined in several ways: exemption or liberation from control by another person or some arbitrary power; liberty; independence; ease of performance, openness, unrestrictedness.

Philosophers like to speak of the difference between "freedom from" and "freedom to." "Freedom from" implies absence of coercion. We strive to be free from the will of tyrants, slave drivers, totalitarian states. During World War II there was a popular German song, "die Gedenken sind frei" (thoughts are free); its theme was that no amount of external force could control one's thoughts.

Women naturally want to feel free from such extreme forms of enslavement as forced marriage, rape, or battering. Women want to be free from demeaning judgments keeping them in unfulfilling roles.

"Freedom to"—or liberty—implies more. It involves the power to bring about what is good. This depends not only on the absence of coercion but also on the interior strength to be an instrument of the good; hence it depends on freedom from enslavement to our own psychological complexes or vices. In this sense women hope to develop their talents and virtues to promote improvement in the family, society, and the Church.

Without a philosophy of human nature and clear-cut goals, freedom can become trivial or dangerous. In these cases it is called whimsy or license.

Let us look at some elements in the free personality to see how these can be integrated with the feminine.

Spontaneity

We think of a woman as repressed or conformist if she is unable to act in a spontaneous and daring manner. We do not applaud a woman whose actions are foolhardy or silly, but we very much enjoy the company of a woman with flair.

Consider the contrast between the two main women characters of the popular movie *The Sound of Music.* The sophisticated middle-aged baroness who hopes to marry Captain von Trapp is not only manipulative and fake but also stiff and conformist. Maria is spontaneous, creative, and daring. At first these qualities of the younger woman frighten her somewhat unimaginative employer, but gradually they delight and rejuvenate him.

It is easy to see that spontaneity is an ingredient of feminine charm. It helps prevent natural charm from congealing into studied manipulation.

Strength to Lead

Leaders require the freedom of real strength. The word "leader" should not be interpreted too narrowly. Queens and prime ministers are leaders, but so are mothers. A writer or artist may be a leader, but so is a teacher. Passive, weak, dependent women lack such freedom. Domineering women appear to be strong but really lack inner freedom. It is insecurity that motivates them to try to control persons and situations.

Strength is important for nurturing, warm, feminine qualities to triumph over the fear that comes from weakness. How often in the tragic story of an abortion we find a nice young woman, eager to be

loving, too weak to avoid premarital sex, too frightened to seek the help of her parents, too weak to
suffer the discomfort of pregnancy in order to give
up the baby for adoption, and certainly too fearful
to fend for herself as a single parent. Strength of
character would have complemented her warm dis-
position and helped her to say No to sex or,
afterward, to make the sacrifices necessary to help,
rather than destroy, her baby.

Objectivity

Another aspect of the free personality is objectivity. To use freedom to choose the good, one must
know what is really beneficial in life. Objectivity is
not synonymous with the negative, often masculine,
traits of being cold, overly analytical, and critical.
These personality defects arise not so much from a
love of truth but from the desire to dominate, perhaps because of an exaggerated fear of making
mistakes, or to show superiority.

Without objectivity a woman's choices can often
be unrealistically sentimental or easily influenced
by others. Men sometimes ridicule women's decision-making processes because women do not
always use objective means to arrive at truth. A fine
example would be Lucy Ricardo in "I Love Lucy."
Lucy is full of charm, but this positive feminine trait
gets swamped in her silly lack of realism.

On the other hand, the intuition of women strong
in common sense, and even further, in contact with
the deepest realities, is rich and fruitful. A contrast-
ing television character would be Olivia, the wife and
mother of "The Waltons."

Roots of Freedom

Most women who want to achieve more freedom want to be stronger.

Often we think of strength as a masculine trait. As mentioned in the chapter "Femininity," men on the average are physically bigger and stronger.

In the past, women have been considered members of the "weaker sex." Today some women are battling this stereotype, either pointing to strengths inherent in women's physical and spiritual makeup, or competing in "man's domain." For example, most women live longer than men. Women also have their own kind of strength: the physical potency for nurturing a baby in the womb and at the breast.

What should we make of the issue of strength, then? Let us further explore the polarity of strength and weakness.

Psychologically, some women become tough as they battle against the men in their lives who can be brutal. Because they detest being enslaved or bullied, these women develop their physical and emotional strength to a competitive level, sometimes gaining power at the expense of the feminine qualities of warmth and charm.

Because of the superior muscular strength of men and the subordinate roles women play in many cultures, women strive to triumph over feelings of weakness and vulnerability. A woman realizes that in this process she may have to sacrifice the security—the approval and protection of men—that comes from assuming secondary roles.

As is clear from the chapter on the feminine, it is not my contention that women should not play helping roles; however, women should come to these complementary endeavors with peaceful strength, not servile dependency.

A ghastly case of dependency and vulnerability, which played to a tragic last act, was the center of public attention in 1980. Jean Harris, a successful fifty-six-year-old career woman, presumably killed the man who had been her lover for fourteen years because of his affair with a younger woman. (She had tried first to kill herself.) In a fascinating article about the way American women passionately identified with Jean Harris, writer Erica Abeel pointed out the threat this story poses to the new feminists. Before this event, Jean Harris might have represented the new independent woman that many wish to become. Since she had accepted a lifestyle that was free from commitments—she chose a love affair over "the stodgy realities" of marriage—why was Jean Harris not strong enough to accept the consequences? "In some bottom layer she [Jean Harris] wasn't the modern self-reliant woman she appeared. Later she would lack the resources, toughness, and coolness essential to that role. Harris had the trappings of independence—but they overlaid dangerous residues from the past. Like the inability to make work the sustaining center it must be if you plan to go it alone. Like the tendency to place not work, but a man—*one* man at the center of your life" (Abeel 1981, 50).

In trying to evaluate true versus false strength, let us go a bit more systematically into the negative aspects of vulnerability, so opposed to true freedom.

One form of weakness found sometimes among North American women, but more frequently in certain other cultures, is passivity. In the face of life's difficulties and seemingly inexorable suffering, a woman can adopt an attitude of false resignation—achieving "peace" by expecting little and enduring all. The price paid for male support is total submission.

Of course, such passivity may stimulate negative masculine traits of cruelty. In *No Exit* (1949), Jean-Paul Sartre's anti-hero, Garcin, describes how his wife's servile passivity disgusts him. He commits worse and worse sins against marital love to arouse her anger. Finally, he brings a prostitute right into their spousal bed and forces his wife to serve them breakfast the next morning.

To give up hope like this may seem slavish to women with independent natures, but the motive may not be to idolize the oppressor; it may instead be an attempt to find one's own equilibrium by refusing to react. In the problem of wife battering, defined as "serious and/or repeated physical injury as a result of deliberate assaults by her spouse," we can find passivity reinforced by social inequality (Hilberman 1980, 1337). In 1968 twenty per cent of the population of the United States approved of wife beating, and forty percent of all female homicide victims were killed by their husbands. Why would any woman put up with physical abuse? Many are afraid to leave their homes, not only because their spouses threaten reprisal, but also because they lack support for themselves and their children. Accustomed to defining themselves dependently, they cannot imagine fending for themselves in the outside world.

In religiously oriented women such fears can be hidden by a veneer of "martyrdom" in the name of bearing a cross for the Lord. Instead of fighting against injustice or accepting it valiantly as an offering to God, some "martyrs" instead see passive resignation as less terrifying than taking a stand.

In the middle and upper classes, another form of passivity can be found among parasitic women. Esther Vilar in *The Manipulated Man* (excerpted in Mahowald 1983) humorously describes the way in which many women avoid intellectual challenges and relax into the torpor of repetitive housewifely existence:

> By the age of twelve at the latest, most women have decided to become prostitutes. Or, to put it another way, they have planned a future for themselves which consists of choosing a man and letting him do all the work. In return for his support, they are prepared to let him make use of their vagina at certain given moments. The minute a woman has made this decision she ceases to develop her mind. . . . Rarely using the time she has gained [by the inventions of men to lessen housework] to take an active interest in history, politics, or astrophysics, woman bakes cakes, irons underclothes, and makes ruffles and frills for blouses, or, if she is especially enterprising, covers her bathroom with flower decals.

Bear in mind that this satiric account is not about busy mothers of small children, but leisurely women without children, or women with many helpers.

Germaine Greer in *The Female Eunuch* draws a biting caricature of the stereotype of the fashion ads, a sterile, unreal woman whose only concern is to create an image of glamour:

> In that mysterious dimension where the body meets the soul the stereotype is born

and has her being. . . . To her belongs all that is beautiful. . . . All that exists, exists to beautify her. The sun shines only to burnish her skin and gild her hair; the wind blows only to whip up the color in her cheeks; the sea strives to bathe her; flowers die gladly so that her skin may luxuriate in their essence. . . . Baby seals are battered with staves, unborn lambs ripped from their mothers' wombs, millions of moles, muskrats, squirrels, minks, . . . and other small and lovely creatures die untimely deaths that she might have furs. (Greer 1971, 47)

If passivity is incompletely achieved, a woman may find herself without the strength to act meaningfully in the world, but unable to resign herself to the sufferings that afflict her. Simone de Beauvoir (1952) writes that finding the world menacing, but outside her control, a woman worries instead of acts. Since everything happens to her through the agency of others, she develops a psychology of complaint and rage. Sometimes, because she refuses to assume responsibility, she does not see the world in its complexity, but instead as pure good (herself and those closest to her) versus pure evil ("they").

"Hysteria" in the popular sense of the term—uncontrolled rage—can be a woman's way of constantly accusing those who dominate her. In this aggressive-passive behavior, a woman will make a tremendous fuss so that everyone around must share in her discomfort, yet she never assertively acts to change her bad situation.

Negative feminine intellectual traits such as silliness and naiveté can also be related to passivity. Unwilling to take the trouble to study and analyze the world around her, a woman may instead adopt a set of oversimplified clichés or childish excuses for ignorance. Sometimes very intelligent women lapse into silliness as a ruse to avoid losing masculine affection. It has been shown that many more women than men introduce ideas with "disclaimers," such as, "I really don't know much about this, but here is one idea, just my own opinion," instead of forthrightly and confidently proclaiming an idea. Much more active displays of weakness include clinging, obsession, and idol worship.

Here is how negative intellectual traits can feed into these other negative emotional traits. A woman without a strong focus, according to Edith Stein (1987), tends to nibble in all directions seeking wholeness; she is unable to develop one gift thoroughly because she lacks confidence. Such an uncomfortable state of existence easily propels a woman toward anyone who appears to have direction or power. How thrilling to ride the tail of the comet. How meaningful to be part of the life of a man who is "going somewhere." Freud thought all women lacked libido and could only find fulfillment through living vicariously off the life energies of another—a male, a stronger female, or a child—achieving this by the proximity that comes with slavish devotion.

Negative feminine traits such as manipulativeness come into play here, as the woman seeks to secure the presence of her "idol." Simone de Beauvoir incisively points out that even if the man is asked to give nothing in return for the woman's undying affection, he is still being forced to give up his own freedom of movement to be present to receive the numerous material and emotional gifts the woman wants so much to indulge him with.

Resentment and spite often follow idol worship, once the clay feet become visible. The European psychotherapist Ida Gorres says that to men, women seem like prowling time bombs. Tied to a particular man as his lover, wife, secretary, or assistant, the disappointed woman seeks ways to vent her anger at his failure to live up to her dreams of his perfection. The love relationships of some male homosexuals, those of an effeminate nature, display similar patterns.

In extreme cases, a woman's sense of self becomes so deficient, through years of dependence, that she will decide to commit suicide if she is threatened with the loss of her worshipped male idol. Of course, there can be other reasons (such as abandonment in early childhood) why the loss of a love object can seem devastating. In any case, how tragic to throw away the whole world with all its beauty, goodness, and promise for the love of one puny mortal! Rightly, a psychologist dealing with a patient, female or male, who wants to take his own life because of unrequited love, looks not at the cruelty of the rejecting party, but at the lack of self-esteem and the narrowness of emotional focus of the suicidal person.

Given such shipwreck, is it any wonder that people try to hide their vulnerability behind a mask of pseudo-strength?

Two principal contemporary ideologies seek to strengthen women in their battle against their own feelings of weakness: feminism and the wholeness theory. We will explore these philosophies and their practical applications, and we will cite relevant thinkers of the past. These two movements will also be evaluated for their positive and negative features.

4
Feminism

The word "feminism" is somewhat ambiguous. Linked to the phrase "women's liberation," it seems to signify the desire to defend the rights of women against various subtle and extreme forms of oppression, such as battering and sexual abuse. Now in the nineties it is possible to distinguish among feminist viewpoints ranging from radical stances insisting that women separate themselves from men completely in society and in churches to women who seek public support for a family income so that all mothers can stay home. While most feminists accept abortion as a necessary option, some call themselves pro-life feminists, viewing all abortion as anti-woman.

In this chapter all these positions will be considered and evaluated.

It should be noted that, at first, the woman's liberation movement of the late sixties and early seventies appeared simply to be the rejection of all societal forms of masculine exploitation of women. It emphasized replacing the enslavement of roles determined by gender with the freedom to choose whatever one might want to do in life.

Gradually a distinction was made between moderate feminism and radical feminism. The latter insisted on more extreme measures to end oppression, such as the abolition of marriage and even of sexual relations with men.

Simultaneously there arose a different, if sympathetic, branch of feminism that emphasized the affirmation of feminine values and lobbied for social reform in consonance with those values. An analogy can be made here with the evolution of the black movement in America. At first, liberation meant gaining equal rights with the majority white population. Then a current developed within the leadership emphasizing "Black is beautiful." Their goal was not to become like "whitey" but instead to delight in what was different in black appearance and culture.

So too, a branch of feminism has arisen that stresses that what is distinctly feminine is beautiful. With this idea came a desire to see society foster such womanly values as motherhood. Maternity leave, for instance, is an idea designed to support the special childbearing function of the female body, rather than view it as a liability.

However, the idea that women have dignity and rights was not invented by the women's liberation movement in the nineteenth century.

Philosophies of Woman

In the fifth century B.C. Plato wrote his dialogue the *Symposium*, which includes his famous myth about the sexes. According to the myth, human beings used to be both male and female in the same entity. But then they were separated into distinct male and female beings, and ever since have sought longingly for their missing halves. This accounts for the vehemence of the sex drive.

Plato developed his most revolutionary ideas about women in Book V of the *Republic.* Equal in mind, women were to have equal educational opportunities and roles, including military service. He thought it desirable to devise a system of communal wives that included eugenic child breeding and permitted promiscuity after the time of fertility had passed. Women were not to be confined to domesticity, but to participate in all aspects of society according to their abilities.

After he tried without success to create his utopia, Plato wrote the *Laws,* in which he reverted to a more complementary theory. What makes for order and purity in society is the feminine, and what leads to majesty and valor comes from the masculine. However, even in this second plan for society, Plato still wanted men and women both to learn gymnastics and horseback riding. Women were not to be treated like slaves. They were not to live softly and waste money, but instead to have reasonable order in their lives.

The first woman philosopher to write about the feminine, as far as we know, was Mary Wollstonecraft, an English woman of the eighteenth century. In *A Vindication of the Rights of Women,* Wollstonecraft tried to prove that what we have been calling negative feminine traits, far from being innate, are the result of the mores of society. Once these have been changed, the great positive virtues of women will emerge more and more clearly, as well as their equal claims to rationality, and hence to equal rights.

"It is time to separate unchangeable morals from local manners," Wollstonecraft wrote, and to her, morality meant living according to Christian standards of virtue (Rossi 1973, 58). But to be ethical, a woman needed a kind of education different from the smattering that girls picked up in her day. She needed to understand principles, acquire rigor, and discover causes rather than observe effects. Cool reason had to replace the reign of irrational romantic love.

Wollstonecraft believed that the kindly feminine traits should come from true love, not submissive dependence. By means of a thorough intellectual and religious education, a woman would be as independent of spirit as a man, able to be a respected friend and confidante rather than a charming plaything. Such an upbringing would also make her a much better wife and mother.

In the nineteenth century John Stuart Mill helped pave the way for English feminism. In his essay *On Liberty* (excerpted in Mahowald 1983), Mill wrote that the real character of women is unknown since it has been so distorted by male philosophers with exploitative natures. It is to their advantage to teach women that they should live only for their husbands and children!

Although in Mill's time women were treated like the body servants of despots, he looked forward to an age when marriage would be a union of equals. Indeed, in his own marriage to an intellectual, equal rights were respected.

Although he thought most women would still want to be wives and mothers even if the customs of society did not force this upon them, he thought it a loss to society if women were not able to exercise their other intellectual and creative faculties.

Mill agreed with his critics that women tended to be more intuitive than principled, but he taught that such imbalance was not innate but rather the result of an education deficient in analytic training. If there are few famous women in history, he noted, it is not due to lack of talent, but rather because women are bogged down with other duties.

Male supremacy has many disadvantages for society. Because of it, Mill argued, men grow to be arrogant and overbearing; the world loses the talents of women; mothers, brought up themselves without a sufficient philosophical foundation, become poor educators of their own children; women keep men back from nonconformist activities for the reform of society because women lack the breadth of vision to understand the needs of their times; social life becomes too dualistic, preventing the cross-fertilization of ideas from both sexes.

At the end of the nineteenth century we find much agitation for women's rights. Marxists stressed the way economic conditions lead to the exploitation of women. Engels wrote a long essay on the "Origin of the Family" (excerpted in Mahowald 1983), and Lenin's commentary was collected into a book entitled *The Emancipation of Women* (excerpted in Mahowald 1983). Engels thought that the women of the proletariat, even if they worked, were still domestic slaves and that the only way to bring about real equality was to abolish the family unit.

The women's suffrage movement became more militant in the early part of the twentieth century. In England such women as Emmeline Pankhurst chose to go to prison as a protest against the slowness of reform. Originally viewed as a proof of the silly naiveté of women, this movement eventually proved the strength of its proponents.

The movement flourished also in the United States. Elizabeth Stanton and Lucretia Mott were already fighting for women's rights in 1848. Later, Susan B. Anthony became the leader. It is hard for us today to believe that basic rights including voting and property ownership were denied solely because of sex for so many centuries.

I mention these historical notes because some antifeminists in our time act as if there never were a problem; they believe that feminism is only the ravings of crazed modern women.

Negative Philosophies of Woman

Feminists today take courage from egalitarian ideas of the past. But today's feminists are also motivated by rage at the negativity toward women expressed by male thinkers throughout the history of Western philosophy and culture.

Although some of the most frequently quoted excerpts that demonstrate this bias are taken out of context and can be nuanced by other quotations, it is important to refer to a few to see how they cause feminist ire.

Aristotle, a disciple of Plato, was convinced that women are inferior to men. In *Generation of Animals* he wrote: "A female is a defective male." In *Poetics* he wrote that it was unseemly to portray a woman as manly or clever. (Both are excerpted in Mahowald 1983.)

Rousseau explains in *Emile* that men should be active and strong; women passive, weak, and pleasing to men.

In "On Women" from *Studies in Pessimism* (excerpted in Mahowald 1983), Schopenhauer describes men as objective and strong, but women as unable to perform anything requiring great labor. She pays her debt to life by suffering, sacrifice, and submission. Men are capable of keen joys and sorrows, women of more trivial things. Men are adults, women are big children. Men are able to consider the past and future and hence develop the virtues of prudence and justice. Men are in every respect superior to women. Men, their reason clouded by sexual desire, foolishly think of women as the fairer sex, whereas in actuality women are "undersized, narrow-shouldered, broad-hipped, and short-legged." According to Schopenhauer, women are rightly called the second sex, "inferior in every respect to the first." They should be denied legal rights.

Nietzsche composed such aphorisms as "Thou goest to women? Remember thy whip!" And, "When a woman has scholarly inclinations there is generally some thing wrong with her sexual nature."

The philosophy of Jean-Paul Sartre, the famous existentialist of our century, presents us with a different, though equally repulsive, manner of describing women. In Sartre's metaphysics nature is seen as absurd, as nauseating. Without God, existence has no meaning. God's creation appears to Sartre only as a sort of slime. Love is viewed as a process of destructive appropriation of the freedom of another; sex is seen as nothing but the emission of slimy substances for the relief of physical pressure. Here is a vivid description of slime as characteristic of all nature, and peculiarly of feminine nature:

> I open my hands, I want to let go of the slimy and it sticks to me, it draws me, it sucks at me. . . . It is a soft, yielding action, a moist and feminine sucking, it lives obscurely under

my fingers, and I sense it like a dizziness; it draws me to it as the bottom of a precipice might draw me. . . .

Slime is the revenge of the In-itself [unconscious being]. A sickly-sweet, feminine revenge which will be symbolized on another level by the quality "sugary." . . . A sugary sliminess is the ideal of the slimy; it symbolizes the sugary death of the For-itself [conscious being] (like that of the wasp which sinks into the jam and drowns in it). (Sartre 1992, 776–777)

Further on in the same section of his existential metaphysical tome, *Being and Nothingness,* Sartre again describes his perception of the feminine:

Here at its origin we grasp one of the most fundamental tendencies of human reality— the tendency to fill. . . . A good part of our life is passed in plugging up holes, in filling empty places, in realizing and symbolically establishing a plenitude. . . .

It is only from this standpoint that we can pass on to sexuality. The obscenity of the feminine sex is that of everything which "gapes open." It is *an appeal to being* as all holes are. In herself woman appeals to a strange flesh which is to transform her into a fullness of being by penetration and dissolution. Conversely woman senses her condition as an appeal precisely because she is "in the form of a hole". . . . Beyond any doubt her sex is a mouth and a voracious mouth which devours the penis—a fact which can easily lead to the idea of castration. The amorous act is the castration of the man; but this is above all because sex is a hole. We have to do here with a *pre-sexual* contribution which will become one of the components of sexuality as an empirical, complex, human attitude but which far from deriving its origin from the sexed being has nothing in common with basic sexuality. . . . Nevertheless the experience with the hole . . . includes the ontological presentiment of sexual experience in general. . . . The hole, before all sexual specification, is an obscene expectation, an appeal to the flesh. (Sartre 1992, 781–2)

I include Sartre's horrifying description of the feminine to show that rejection of God and nature can lead to rejection of the feminine nature.

Roots of Twentieth-Century Feminism

The most outstanding feminist voice of the twentieth century is the oft-quoted Simone de Beauvoir. Here is de Beauvoir's concise relation of her metaphysics to the plight of woman: Man transcends Life through existence; by this he creates values that deprive pure repetition of all value. In animals the freedom and variety of male activities are vain because no project is involved. All is for the species. The human male remodels the face of the earth and shapes the future. The woman celebrates in festivals the victory of the males. Her misfortune is to have been biologically destined for the repetition of Life when even her own view of Life does not carry within itself its reason for being, reasons that are more important than the life itself (see de Beauvoir 1952, 59).

In other words, de Beauvoir thinks that having babies is merely a repetition, while men are able to do something new and original through their projects. (Clearly, such a view differs tremendously from the "naive" opinion of many mothers: procreating a new human being is the greatest experience in life!) Throughout *The Second Sex,* de Beauvoir contends that masculinity is the favored type, and femininity is secondary.

Women are afraid to risk establishing their own identity, and hence in their complicity with male dominance they develop the traits that work to the male's advantage. Men like to think women are happy in their stagnation. They delight in poetic images of the eternal feminine to conceal the monotony of maternity and domesticity.

Ethically, de Beauvoir rejects anything that continues the limiting conditions of the past and present. She links freedom with the search for change and identifies such liberty with the masculine personality. Women must be freed so that they can engage in projects of their own choice, without being subordinate to the men who surround them. The emancipated woman wants to be a taker and a doer, not a passive object of male needs.

Yet, de Beauvoir says, the contemporary woman finds herself in an ambiguous position. On the one hand she wants to hold on to her feminine ways of manipulating men, and on the other she wants to assert her equal transcendence.

It would seem that de Beauvoir's solution to the tension between femininity and freedom is to opt for freedom and get rid of the feminine, both positive and negative. However, a close reading of *The Second Sex* shows that it is primarily the negative feminine that she rejects. She endorses the positive feminine, provided it is not viewed as innate but as a choice. Her metaphysics rejects the concept of creation as a gift.

De Beauvoir's ideal is comradeship between men and women. This can be effected not merely by economic changes, but by embodying new values in cultural forms such as family and education. This will eliminate feminine dependence and inferiority, but need not banish "love, happiness, poetry, dream."

The book that triggered the women's liberation movement in the United States was *The Feminine Mystique*, written in 1963 by Betty Friedan. This best-selling paperback described the frustrations of middle-class suburban housewives. The anger it created in women who were jerked out of their passivity by Friedan's depiction of their plight helped to swell the numbers who would eventually support the more militant aims of such women's liberation organizations as NOW.

Let's consider some of Friedan's ideas in "Our Revolution is Unique" (excerpted in Mahowald 1983), written after her own movement had split—the more radical members claiming Friedan was too moderate.

"Man is not the enemy, but the fellow victim of the present half-equality." His residual negativity deprives him of the sensitivity and tenderness he himself longs to express.

On the subject of sex and related issues, Friedan claims that women will only cease to be sex objects "when [they] are . . . liberated to a creativity beyond motherhood, to a full human creativity." Motherhood is good, but only when chosen freely. The right to contraceptives and abortion is crucial for the liberation of women.

However, Friedan's controversial and, to me, horrifying, acceptance of contraception and abortion as essential elements in a feminist program seems like a mild voice in comparison to her radical sisters.

For instance, some radical feminist writers think that the institution of marriage "protects" women in the same way that the institution of slavery was said to "protect" blacks—that is, the word "protection" in this case is simply a euphemism for oppression. Freedom for women cannot be won without abolition of marriage (Koedt and Firestone 1971).

The articles in the second year's annual of the same series develop this theme. Whereas personalists show that it is only self-donation in love that leads to fulfillment, radical feminists think it is necessary to destroy love, for love prevents the full development of a woman's human potential by directing all her energies outward to the interests of others.

As we discuss increasingly extreme variations on the theme of radical change, you will note the vehemence of tone, culminating in manifestos where the proliferation of four-letter words (negative masculine?) requires some omissions to avoid offense.

Let me begin with the ideas of Ti-Grace Atkinson from *Amazon Odyssey* (excerpted in Mahowald 1983). Traditional feminism failed, Atkinson theorizes, because it didn't get to the root of the problem—the tendency of women to define themselves in the terms of masculine society. What is needed is for women to "eradicate their own definition. Women must, in a sense, commit suicide. . . . As women begin massing together, they take the first step from *being* massacred to *engaging in* battle (resistance). Hopefully this will eventually lead to negotiations—in the very far future—and peace."

This was written in the sixties. When she resigned from NOW Atkinson thought that women must reject marriage and love and sex as well. In this way women can begin to define themselves without reference to being the "wife man of a husband or the suckler [female] of a baby."

It is not men who must be destroyed but rather their learned roles—oppressive roles which she describes as "metaphysical cannibalism," that is, the appropriation of women into a slave position. Why do men try to cannibalize women? All people—men and women—feel frustrated by their own lack of complete power and so they seek to gain some degree of control through enslaving others. In the case of men, the exploitation is direct, for a man can literally enter a woman and occupy her body. This is always a form of rape, according to Atkinson.

How can a woman escape such tyranny? Does she even wish to? Atkinson describes woman's traditional way of avoiding confrontation with her weak passivity as "the psychopathological condition of love."

It is a euphoric state of fantasy in which the victim transforms her oppressor into her redeemer. She turns her natural hostility toward the aggressor against the remnants of herself—her Consciousness—and sees her counterpart in contrast to herself as all-powerful (as he is by now at her expense). . . .

What is . . . necessary is for the Oppressed to cure themselves (destroy the female role), to throw off the Oppressor, and to help the

Oppressor to cure himself (to destroy the male role).

Selections from a chapter in the anthology *Masculine/Feminine,* edited by Betty and Theodore Roszak (1969), give expression to a feminism increasingly dominated by negative masculine rhetoric and suggest that the only way to overcome weakness and to be free is to become brutal.

The WITCH Manifesto

On Halloween 1963 feminists dressed as witches descended on the New York Stock Exchange heaping curses and spells upon high finance and singing a song especially written for the occasion, "Up Against the Wall Street." "The WITCH Manifesto" is another expression of this vociferous and theatrical group—or should we say coven?

WITCH is in all women, everything.
It's theatre, revolution,
Magic, terror and joy.
It's an awareness that witches and gypsies
Were the first guerrillas and resistance fighters
Against oppression—the oppression of women,
Down through the ages.
Witches have always been women who dared
To be groovy, courageous, aggressive,
Intelligent, non-conformist, explorative,
Independent, sexually liberated, and revolu-
      tionary.
(This may explain why nine million women
Have been burned as witches.)
Witches were the first friendly heads
      and dealers,
The first birth-control practitioners,
      and abortionists,
The first alchemists.

They bowed to no man,
Being the last living remnants
Of the oldest culture of all—
One in which men and women are equal
sharers in a truly cooperative society,
Before the death-dealing sexual,
Economic, and spiritual repression
Of the "Imperialist Phallic Society"
Took over and began to s—— all over nature,
And human life.
A witch lives and laughs in every woman.
She is the free part of each of us,
Beneath the shy smiles,
The acquiescence to absurd male domination,
The make-up of flesh-suffocating clothing
Our sick society demands.
There is no joining WITCH.
If you are a woman, and dare to look within
    yourself,
You are a witch.
You make your own rules.
You are free and beautiful.
You can be invisible or evident,
In how you choose to make your witch self
    known.
You can form your own Coven of sister witches.
Do your own actions.
Whatever is repressive,
Solely male-oriented,
Greedy, puritanical, authoritarian,
Those are your targets,
Your weapons are theatre,
Magic, satire, explosions, herbs,
Music, costumes, masks, stickers,
Paint, brooms, voodoo dolls,
Cats, candles, bells,

Your boundless beautiful imagination.
Your power comes from your own self,
As a woman.
From sharing, rapping, and acting
In concert with your sisters.
You are pledged to free our brothers
From oppression and stereotyped sexual roles,
as well as ourselves.
You are a witch by being female,
Untamed, angry, joyous, and immortal.
You are a witch by saying aloud
"I am a witch"
And thinking about that.

If this manifesto seems so utterly wild to you that you would never expect to meet anyone with such views, consider that *some,* though certainly not all, Christian feminists wish to introduce pagan symbols into the Mass. One conference calling itself "Christian feminist" ended with a liberating dance by all those present who exulted in their lesbianism.

One last "gem" comes from "The Bitch Manifesto" (anonymous 1969 [unpublished]), and it is included to indicate an extreme of how feminist assertiveness might manifest itself as an antidote to passivity:

Bitches are aggressive, assertive, domineering, overbearing, strong-minded, spiteful, hostile, direct, blunt, candid, obnoxious, thick-skinned, hard-headed, vicious, dogmatic, competent, competitive, pushy, independent, stubborn, demanding, manipulative, egoistic, driven, achieving, overwhelming, threatening, scary, ambitious, tough, brassy, masculine, boisterous, and turbulent. Among other things, a Bitch occupies a lot of psychological space. You always know when she is around. . . . You may not like her, but you cannot ignore her.

Some women are emerging bankrupt from these radical movements. Fortunately they are turning to philosophies of woman with greater promise of true fulfillment.

Pro-life Feminism

Only after the first edition of *Feminine, Free, and Faithful* was printed did I become familiar enough with pro-life and Christian feminism to include sections on them in this chapter.

In the anthology of articles called *Pro-Life Feminism* (see Bibliography for other data on this), we find the manifesto of this fascinating confluence of views of social justice activists and anti-abortion heroines of the Operation Rescue movement:

> Two great social movements have been evolving during the Seventies, the pro-life movement and the women's movement. Tragically, they are perceived as opposing movements. Many pro-life people fear equality for women as a dark threat to the family. Many feminists are willing to suffer the killing of their unborn daughters and sons in the name of an elusive freedom. But feminists also believe in family; pro-lifers cherish freedom.
>
> The pro-life tenet is that each and every human being, pre-born or born, deserves the opportunity to develop into the best she or he is capable of; that each individual be respected, however minimal or great their development may be. (Paulette Joyer, "Pro-Life

and Feminism: No Opposition" [from *Pro-Life Feminism,* 1])

Pro-life feminists insist that if women want equal rights they must stand up for the equal rights of the unborn. They must also come against the male irresponsibility involved in abortion and its heavy consequences as the penalty imposed by male indifference to the mother of his child. Pro-life feminists deplore the way the mostly-male abortion establishment has profited from keeping women ignorant of the true nature of abortion.

Many women initially think of abortion not as male exploitation but rather as their own form of liberation. Pro-life ministries devoted to healing of the terrible emotional after-effects of abortion, some of which only come to consciousness years afterwards, stress how confused most women are during the panic that often accompanies the decision to abort. Women suffering from guilt are urged to seek sacramental confession, support groups, and counseling.

Christian Feminism

Since the 1970s Christian feminism has assumed more prominence with a greater range of platforms. In general, the work of Christian feminism deals with the many ways that a presumably patriarchal (male-dominated) Church has worked to suppress women's gifts and contributed to injustices of the worst kinds against women's dignity and rights.

At first such claims led to moderate reform programs such as affirming greater leadership of women in the Church, or recommending more reading of women saints and mystics to balance theological writings of a more analytic masculine style. Many women in the Church who had no more radical agenda than this still call themselves Christian feminists.

By the eighties, however, more revolutionary ideas came to be included under the name of Christian feminism, and were embraced not only by women theologians but also less-educated women. At workshops and conferences and retreats, ideas were circulated which included calling God "she," arranging for "masses" presided over by women "priests," and leaving the Church body to form "woman churches." In some cases there has been a rejection of perennial Christian moral teachings on extra-marital sex, contraception, abortion (under certain conditions), divorce and remarriage without Church annulment or dispensation, and lesbian sexual expression.

In her book *Ungodly Rage: The Hidden Face of Catholic Feminism,* Donna Steichen offers innumerable examples from writings and workshops of radical feminists to demonstrate the destructive nature of this type of feminism.

Scripture scholar Francis Martin thoroughly evaluates the theological premises of Christian feminist theology in *The Feminist Question.* He quotes extensively from such feminist theologians as Anne Carr, Mary Daly, Rosemary Radford Reuther, Elisabeth Schussler-Fiorenza, and Sandra Schneiders. Martin believes that the feminist movement can provide a helpful challenge to the Church in *some* of its platforms; nevertheless, he demonstrates how *most* Christian feminists construct a theology that does away with the revelatory and normative character of Scripture. Feminist theologians, he explains, evaluate religious experience and practice on the basis of their own perspective instead of according to the truths given by the Father through Christ and the Holy Spirit.

More specific ideas of Christian feminists will follow in a later section of this book.

The Truths of Feminism

While feminism, particularly radical feminism, has many negative aspects, it contains some truths. I believe that as Christians it is our duty to search out these truths and utilize them for the betterment of the Church and society.

Some evidence of the Church's desire to affirm the truths in feminism is a report of the World Synod of Catholic Bishops of 1980 (*Origins*, Oct. 23, 1980), which includes the following points:

> In point of fact, there is no reputable theologian today who would deny that the equality of man and woman is constituted by God and confirmed by Christian teaching. . . .

> In many cultures women are discriminated against in one way or another and left in a subservient position. Men, on the other hand, are also often forced to assume dominant and competitive roles. . . .

> At the same time, under the influence of the Holy Spirit, people around the world are becoming more and more sensitive to the dignity of each person, regardless of sex, creed and race, recognizing the person's innate right to respect and freedom from unjust oppression. . . .

> The state of submission and oppression which women are subjected to in the world is a sinful situation, the result of original sin... therefore something to correct.

Additional evidence for the Church's positive attitude toward its female members can be found in writings dating from the first century through the twentieth century A.D. For example, the earliest Christian writings show that the Virgin Mary has been held in great esteem since the time of Christ's ministry on earth.

In our day evidence is most prevalent and most profound in the writings and actions of Pope John Paul II, particularly his apostolic letter *Mulieris Dignitatem* ("On the Dignity and Vocation of Women") and his catechetical work *The Original Unity of Man and Woman.* Even so, it is currently in vogue among feminists and those influenced by them to cry out that the Pope perpetuates sexist attitudes. I will address this issue in greater detail in my section on Faithfulness.

Along those lines, I see the following as the truths in feminism which we cannot ignore: the recognition of the equal dignity of persons, leading to rejection of the negative masculine exploitation of women; the rejection of the negative feminine with all its degrading compromises; the recognition of individual freedom, leading to rejection of stereotyping; and the need for positive social change.

Both the feminist movement and the hippie movement of the sixties and seventies contributed toward exposing the evils of negative masculine traits, such as domineering, smug, and patronizing attitudes. Men eager to show their rejection of the negative masculine are quick to volunteer to pour coffee at a meeting, to plan the menu, and to cook. Fewer now refer to middle-aged women as girls. Many more men share family duties with their working wives. Men are learning the value of showing emotion and vulnerability. I also applaud feminism's rejection of certain aspects of the negative feminine such as over dependence, silliness, coyness, naiveté, manipulativeness, random seductiveness, and compulsive chatter.

Today's society needs strong women. Weak feminine types may be charming in certain respects, but not in these embattled times.

In her work on woman's education, the Catholic philosopher Edith Stein wrote that by nature women have the gifts to pursue non-domestic tasks.

> The fact that *all* powers which the husband possesses are present in feminine nature as well—even though they may generally appear in different degrees and relationships—is an indication they should be employed in corresponding activity. And wherever the circle of domestic duties is too narrow for the wife to attain the full formation of her powers, both nature and reason concur that she reach out beyond this circle. It appears to me, however, that there is a limit to such professional activities whenever it jeopardizes domestic life, i.e., the community of life and formation consisting of parents and children. (Stein 1987, 79)

I particularly appreciate today's emphasis on the individual woman and her special talents, some results of feminist pressure. I personally have no great interest in traditionally masculine sports, but why not delight when other women enjoy them and can successfully compete? As Simone de Beauvoir correctly perceived, girls do not climb trees to be equal to boys, but because it's fun! Why shouldn't women logicians, engineers, or doctors follow their natural bents? In the past, women with temperaments less suited to the duties of life in the home were often reduced to seething resentment, as they felt forced to fulfill hated tasks day after day.

Without agreeing with those feminists who think of full-time daycare as the career mom's final solution, I do believe that feminist social programs can benefit a woman who has to or wants to combine motherhood with other work or activities on a part-time basis. Seeking *help* with the children is altogether different from seeking a *substitute* for the mother.

In my classes in philosophy of woman I find that the issue of motherhood versus career is the greatest cause of stress for my women students. Many think that there is no way to combine both a career and motherhood; they fantasize that they can achieve some kind of perfection only if they pursue one or the other without distraction. Hence they face these frightening alternatives: either pursue a career and use contraceptives or abortion, experiencing uncreative sexual pleasure along the way; or choose the mother role and squelch their desire for other forms of self-expression.

When my husband became disabled I felt obliged to work full time to support the family. At the time this seemed not so much an option as a necessity. Since that time, however, studies have produced so much evidence of the ill-effects on children of having mothers working full time outside the home, that I think that if I had it all to do over I might have chosen part-time work supplemented by some kind of state assistance.

So far has the pendulum swung toward women working full time outside the home that any advice about ways of combining motherhood and career always needs to be preceded by great emphasis on the goodness of homemaking and child-raising by the mother. In Catholic teachings such as *Familiaris Consortio,* the family is understood as a communion of persons. Love in the family is a much higher value than work outside the home for those with a family vocation. This image stands in contradiction to modern patterns in which the house often becomes a sort of launching pad for the members to go out into the world to seek fulfillment outside the family.

In her book *Can Motherhood Survive?* Connie Marshner shows how disastrous it can be when tiny and older children are sent out to daycare centers for reasons no more compelling than the greater stimulation of career over motherhood. And taking the issue one step further she shows how biblical tradition supports the goodness of life in the home for women. Quoting from Proverbs 31, she comments in this way about the fulfilled woman:

> *The heart of her husband doth safely trust in her:* She has a good two-way relationship, based on adult trust.
>
> *She seeketh wool and flax and worketh willingly with her hands:* She is in charge of the spinning and weaving and works along with the others at it.
>
> *She is like the merchants' ships; she bringeth her food from afar:* She's a bargain hunter, who shops at more than one store.
>
> *She riseth also while it is yet night, and giveth meat to her household, and a portion to her*

maidens: No idler, she gets breakfast ready before anybody is up, even the servants, for whom she is responsible.

She considereth a field, and buyeth it: with the fruit of her hands she planteth a vineyard: Her experience and shrewdness add to the family wealth; maybe the money she made from selling cheese, she saves until she can buy a vineyard. No helpless "I can't balance the checkbook" type, this woman. . . .

She stretcheth out her hand to the poor; yea, she reacheth forth her hands to the needy: Not only does she manage the family and participate in the family enterprise, but she also initiates charitable acts.

She maketh fine linen, and selleth it: She has a cottage industry on the side.

She openeth her mouth with wisdom, and in her tongue is the law of kindness: She is not ignorant or uninformed about current affairs, but not trying to be "one of the boys" either.

Her children arise up, and call her blessed; her husband also, and he praiseth her: In the course of contributing to the family prosperity, she did not fail to raise her children right. They were not neglected; they love her. And so does her husband.

Give her of the fruit of her hands; and let her own works praise her in the gates: No need to hide her light under a bushel; let her accomplishments speak for themselves; let her enjoy the fruit of her accomplishments. (139)

Given this ideal, what are we to say about single mothers, or those married women whose circumstances or legitimate interests make work outside the home necessary or desirable? Are they bad mothers? Such is not Catholic teaching. Yes, the mother at home is the ideal, but there can be real heroism in other choices, especially when they are motivated by love for the family or a response to talents that are God-given and may constitute a special vocation. After all, there were women saints who left their families in the care of others to pursue works of God. More commonly, a single mother or a woman without whose supplemental income the family could not live in a safe neighborhood is willing to undertake the great burden of double work, inside and outside the home. Even at work such a woman's heart is with her beloved family, as Alice von Hildebrand likes to say.

Some mothers faced with such choices decide to devote themselves all day and night to their children through their pre-school years, but then seek full-time work for pay after the children are in school. Some have found good ways to supplement needed income by work done at home, such as computer programming. To avoid sending little children to institutions for daycare many mothers prefer to bring someone into the home as a helper or to rely on relatives or close friends for shared child-care rotation.

Sometimes a mother can avoid being gone all day by the family's adoption of a much simpler lifestyle, with older children taking on part-time work. The "simpler lifestyle" option is often too easily dismissed even by Christians in our consumer-oriented society.

Much prayer and discernment and counsel should accompany such decisions.

Falsehoods and False Values of Feminism

My critique of feminism will include the following main points: most feminism uses the masculine as a model, thereby underrating the positive feminine; while early feminists considered abortion a result of the negative masculine irresponsibility of the male, most contemporary feminists endorse this act, which is the most rampant abuse of the innocent in our society today; lastly, most feminism lacks a philosophy of the person in which to ground the positive feminine.

In my comments on the ideas of radical feminists, I have already begun to indicate the distressing manner in which women, originally protesting negative masculine traits in men, now slide into recommending them for women.

Christine Garside Allen, in an unpublished article "True Sex-Polarity," mentions that in all revolutions there can be distortions, especially when the newly freed group takes on the characteristics of the oppressor. In this case, the revolution commits suicide.

We are all familiar with the increasing number of aggressive, shrewd, cold, and domineering women in our society since the promotion of militant feminism.

Contemporary norms in the education and acculturation of women can also present the problem of the disparagement of the positive feminine in terms of the development of positive and negative masculine qualities.

Many times the legitimate seeking of equality leads to a sameness of education, often, though not always, along masculine lines. More women are being steered into fields previously dominated by men, than men are being encouraged to study homemaking skills. To trace this idea back to its foundation in feminism, consider this: Why does de Beauvoir see interior decorating as drudgery yet building a community fountain, say, as exhilarating? Psychologist Judith Bardwick (1979) writes that women too often internalize male roles and their criteria for success and achievement such as competence, risk-taking, and competitiveness. Instead, we might be judging ourselves on how cooperative we are, how willing to affirm others in a work situation, as some feminists do recommend.

Ethical issues related to feminism are significantly related to the depreciation of the positive feminine coming out of the women's liberation movement. According to Samuel Blumenfeld in his book *The Retreat from Motherhood* (1975), 1973 saw the lowest birthrate and the highest divorce rate in the history of America. Women are losing the sense of the privilege of motherhood. He suggests also that men often support women's liberation because it allows them to be more irresponsible. Persuaded that marriage and family life are imprisoning, women will not wait for marriage for their sexual fulfillment.

Browsing through a stationery store one day, I was struck by the amount of space devoted to the sale of stuffed animals—nearly half the store. I noticed that girls and women, after buying these cute toys, would hug them to their breasts. Some women I know have whole beds full of individually named stuffed animals on which they lavish the affection they might be extending to the live babies they have rejected by contraception and abortion.

In a kind of manifesto, I once wrote: I long for the day when feminists will realize that equal rights for women need not be accompanied by negation of the distinctly feminine.

What kind of freedom is it that insists on using contraceptive devices harmful to women's bodies and often also abortifacient?

Doesn't it show more self-love and strength to demand that men respect the special fertile time when we are potential mothers?

I would like to see the day when knowledge of our own natural cycles will enable us to proclaim with pride, "This week I am a potential miracle worker. Come to me with your seed only if you want to be part of this wonder by becoming a father!"

I would like to see the day when no woman would punish herself, her man, or her baby by abortion, but would instead cherish her own womb and its fruit. For isn't abortion a form of stereotyping when it speaks of unwanted babies instead of affirming the uniqueness of each baby? And is it not an extreme form of negative masculine control to pass a death sentence on a helpless infant because he or she will not be an asset at this time? I would like to see the day when all women would avail themselves of the help offered by the pro-life community to overcome any financial, psychological, or other difficulties that stand in the way of completing their motherhood.

I would like to see "sisterhood become powerful": women who could not raise their children would bear them courageously to give to their nonfertile sisters in adoption. I would like to see women working together for maternity and paternity leave, for better daycare, and for creative ways to combine motherhood and careers.

Is true feminism anti life? No. Can a feminist support the Human Life Amendment? Yes. As a wife, mother, and professional woman I look forward to the day when all women will see that affirming their own lives means affirming the lives of all, no matter how small!

Correcting the Defects of Feminism

Are the defects of feminism correctable? It's a controversial question. As I hinted at in my section *The Truths of Feminism*, I do believe that there can be a philosophy of woman that includes feminism's valid insights about freedom. But such a viewpoint would have to include a metaphysical foundation in which to ground the positive feminine.

Let me try to explain what I mean in simple terms. All values find their home in the nature of reality. Freedom depends on objectivity. Our theoretical notion of what is the most basic meaning of life enables us to sort out various values and determine priorities.

If, for example, the meaning of life is self-fulfillment through the development of one's physical, intellectual, and artistic abilities—exclusively—then the development of positive feminine values is but a possibility; such values will be considered good if they foster individuality, bad if they impede it.

But suppose, instead, that the meaning of life is growth in love. Then the experiences of the heart in most intimate relationships will be of equal if not superior value to cultivation of other gifts; and, for a woman, the use of her special forms of relating will be cherished as prime. She will want not only freedom to choose, but liberty to have strength to sustain womanly roles. And her lovingness will also free the male sex to be responsible and fathering instead of cold and uncaring.

In other words, to be truly free as a woman one must also be feminine and faithful.

5
Jungian Wholeness

Another theory about how to liberate women to greater strength is called *wholeness.* This philosophy is hard to define and survey because it is both relatively new and fertile with insights and combinations. Let me begin by simply defining wholeness theory as it will be used in this chapter. *Wholeness* is a goal of personality growth by which the feminine and masculine components are integrated in both women and men.

Wholeness springs from the perception, developed primarily in Jungian psychology, that many people are one-sided in some respects, including the masculine or feminine. A man might have too much masculine and too little feminine. A woman might have too much feminine and too little masculine. But also a man might have too much feminine or a woman too much masculine. Psychic wholeness comes when such imbalances begin to be rectified by "coming into touch with" the deeply hidden and undeveloped parts of the self.

The discussion of feminine and masculine in Jungian psychology includes two terms, which are still vague and confusing to the uninitiated, the *anima* and the *animus.* These words are not, as some imagine, simply synonyms for feminine and masculine. No; they are more subtle. They are archetypes:

97

inherited modes of psychic functioning that parallel certain instincts in animals.

Anima is the feminine part of a man's nature, unconscious to him, and usually projected; *animus* is the masculine part of a woman's nature. In other words, every man has an archetypal image of the feminine, a highly emotionally charged fantasy symbol. This "feminine principle" is really inside him, but he projects it onto real women, as he tries to find the ideal in the real. In the same way, every woman has an archetypal image of the masculine. This masculine principle is within her, but is projected onto the men she meets, as she seeks the ideal in the real.

Projection ultimately fails, for real men and women cannot satisfy our desire for the perfection of the ideal. However, all is not lost. When during therapy or self-analysis a man or woman realizes the extent of his or her yearning for the feminine or masculine, he or she may begin to search for it within the *self*.

So, for example, if I find myself passionately in love with a man because of his obvious strength, and then become disillusioned when I discover his clay feet, instead of turning against the man in bitterness because he failed to be an adequate leaning post, I can seek the masculine strength I need within my own self.

Or a man enchanted with a delicate, tender woman may feel cheated to discover that she is not a flower but a live human being, capable even of perspiration; instead of punishing her for failing to live up to his image, he can seek the delicate, tender emotions buried within his own psyche, for example, by writing poetry or tending a garden.

How do these ideas about projection of the masculine and feminine relate to wholeness theory? When I begin to be aware of my hidden masculine and feminine qualities, I can try to become whole, or integrated, by getting in touch with these parts. The whole man will then *live out* his masculine and feminine traits. The whole woman will be comfortable with *living out* her feminine and masculine traits.

To make this idea more vivid, think of women and men you admire. Do not most of them have this kind of wholeness? Christian Jungians advise us to meditate on the way that Jesus manifested all the masculine and feminine traits. Was Joan of Arc not passionately responsive and yet also courageous to the death?

Let's see what a Jungian wholeness analyst might think of the process of weak women seeking the roots of freedom through greater strength. M. Esther Harding writes the following:

> Western civilization lays especial emphasis on the value of the outer, and this fits in more nearly with man's nature than with woman's. The feminine spirit is more subjective, more concerned with feelings and relationships than with the laws and principles of the outer world. And so it happens that the conflict between outer and inner is usually more devastating for women than for men. (Harding 1971, 11)

According to Harding, there is a great conflict in women between the masculine side they must develop to work in the world, and their "more ancient feminine nature." For women of our times "a one-sided life is not sufficient; the conflict between the opposing tendencies of masculine and feminine within them must be faced. They cannot resume the feminine values in the old instinctive and unconscious way."

Harding also thinks that modern women are more schooled in the masculine than the feminine and that they will be stronger by relating to their feminine side!

In an interesting chapter in *Woman's Mysteries,* Harding develops the idea of "The Virgin Goddess" as a symbol of a feminine way of being liberated. The virgin goddesses in various religions are not dependent on a human male, but achieve fulfillment by being ravished by their god. Meditation on virgin goddesses can lead women to understand the way in which sacrifices of the ego's desires can be freeing and renewing when our passions are given back to the God to whom we belong. Through the transformation of passion in response to the divine, women can gain sexual control without the unsatisfactory effects of repression. Out of such unconventional sublimation of sexual drives comes the maternal feeling women desire so keenly to experience with a universal scope. In other words, we cannot just repress the negative feminine, for then it will always come back in haunting fantasies and destructive outbreaks. Instead, we must relate to the divine in complete passion and let the divine fertilize us, bringing forth positive feminine traits.

Harding points to the archetype of goddesses who have to sacrifice their sons to help women with the problem of possessiveness. Today women who ponder such symbols will come to understand the primordial meaning of the necessary process of letting go.

A woman healed and integrated through the divine can inspire men without trying to conquer them. If she is married, her *inner* virginity will express itself in her independence of convention and ratification by others. She will be a free spirit or, in Jung's terms, an *individual* who is at home in herself.

Harding's ideas are evocative; but I certainly don't think women should meditate on goddesses. We should ponder instead the fascinating and inspiring archetypes of positive feminine traits in Mary and the women saints.

Receiving Woman, a book by Ann Belford Ulanov (1981), another Jungian therapist and professor of psychiatry and religion at Union Theological Seminary, can further aid our understanding of the ideal of wholeness and feminine strength.

Reacting against the stereotyping of the past and of present-day movements, Ulanov tries to help each woman see herself as an individual with a wide range of possibilities as she combines the masculine and feminine parts of herself.

> Many women are beginning to understand that they can no more be determined in their inmost selves by the old benevolent patriarchy than by the new malevolent sexism. New stereotypes are no less coercive than old ones. No great distance exists between "All real women marry and bear children" and "All real women know that men are sexists and rapists at heart." . . . In both, woman is a passive victim, determined by forces outside herself that she may resist, but is all but helpless to change. (Ulanov 1981, 17)

Unlike Jung, Ulanov objects to the idea that woman experiences her unconscious as masculine in the obverse of the way man finds his unconscious to be feminine. Instead she feels that our concept of the feminine has to expand to include all of what women really are, including intellect, drive, and power.

The idea that women become strong, not by trying to be more masculine, but by allowing their own individual freedom and courage to come forth, is becoming more prevalent among psychologists. After all, gentleness is different in a man than in a woman precisely because it is a powerful man who is being gentle. In the same way, strength in a woman is different precisely because it may overcome passivity.

In *The Woman in the Tower* by Betsy Caprio (1983), a spiritual director and parish minister, women are taught to experiment with possibilities of greater wholeness by getting in touch with the four elements, symbols of Jungian personality types.

Air	=	thinking
Earth	=	sensory
Fire	=	intuition
Water	=	feeling

Caprio resolves a problem regarding the feminine and masculine I have often puzzled over in my study of wholeness theory. If women develop the masculine and men the feminine, why wouldn't their personalities end up being alike? Then it would make no difference whether one was with a woman or a man except biologically! Betsy Caprio theorizes, on the contrary, that for a woman to be whole she must develop her feminine side *first*. The masculine in her must take the form of *inner* strength and not become an aggressive thrust in the world. Likewise, for men, the masculine must be developed first, with the feminine flourishing within, rather than in an outward form of exaggerated feminine traits.

To translate Caprio's image into the categories of this book: the woman would have a strong positive feminine bolstered by an inner positive masculine, and the man would have a strong positive masculine with a beautiful inner positive feminine. If the woman tries to develop the masculine first, she is all too likely to fall into the negative masculine. If the man tries to develop the feminine first, he may slip into the negative feminine.

Jungians also speak of women having different personality types, each with its own strengths. The girlish woman is spontaneous and charming; the interior woman has the strength of wisdom. The motherly woman is enduring; the strong, assertive woman can carry out projects in the world at large. One can gain in wholeness by developing areas of the feminine previously neglected.

Strengths of Wholeness Theory

The truths of wholeness theory seem to jump out at me when I meet an individual who demonstrates a remarkable lack of wholeness: for instance, an extremely negative-masculine man who is cold, domineering, and overly critical; or an extraordinarily negative-feminine woman who is weak, passive, and silly. And so I consider one of the main strengths of wholeness theory the attempt to liberate people from such crippling one-sidedness.

Another benefit of wholeness theory is the reverence its proponents exhibit for the processes going on in the deeper part of others as well as oneself.

Most women are one-sidedly feminine at times; this can severely limit their freedom to bring about the good. In some circumstances feminine warmth, charm, and intuition need the balance of a daring attitude, leadership, and the objectivity that comes from analysis.

The word "process" has become something of a cliché in popular psychology, along with its correlative "growth." Yet we owe a great deal to the thinkers who have developed such concepts. A Christian button worn in the seventies read "Please don't judge me; God isn't finished with me yet."

The belief that others and oneself are not fixed in unsatisfactory patterns, but instead might be in a state of hibernation pending a new spring, helps bring forth new energies. In a Charles Williams novel a sage advises his neophyte that it is a sin to give up on another person, to make a picture of him at his worst moment and then believe that to be the final portrait. Juli Loesch Wiley, columnist for the *National Catholic Register,* often warns against "hard-boiling" people in their sins.

Sister Mary Neill, a Dominican theologian who is well versed in wholeness theory, gives many self-exploration workshops. She uses common images to jostle the psyche out of its rut-like resignation to stagnant patterns. Questions such as "When have you most needed a refuge?" and "When have you been a refuge for others?" gently lead participants into openness to positive feminine and masculine traits. Sister Neill sometimes speaks of those whose personalities seem consolidated around negative characteristics as "not having done their emotional homework."

In other words, we should not think we can become assertive women just by an exercise of will power, but neither should we sink into passivity about our shortcomings.

Reverence for our struggles to achieve wholeness leads us to appreciate the individual instead of insisting on conformity. Proposals for flexible options in society can be offered in a warm, concerned way, rather than in the strident, protesting spirit sometimes displayed by feminists who push the same programs.

Weaknesses of Wholeness Theory

The weaknesses of wholeness theory become apparent when wholeness is considered the sole goal of life. When its insights are instead part of a wider philosophy, especially a Christian perspective, the defects of this psychological school can for the most part be overcome.

The problems I see in wholeness theory include these: insufficient distinction between positive and negative traits, idolization of process and of the individual, vagueness about critical ethical norms.

Some proponents of wholeness theory will refer to certain traits as demonic, but often the interest in overcoming repression takes the form of a fascination with the feminine and masculine without distinguishing between the positive and negative traits of each.

A therapeutic perspective can influence an individual's philosophy in a way that may confuse rather than clarify the issues. Since the unexpressed parts of the personality can explode destructively, therapists may advise clients to experiment with their hidden masculine or feminine. The result can be worse than the original less dynamic, but less harmful, state of being. For example, a masculinized woman may start manifesting her negative feminine by seducing happily married men. A quiet, passive man may become viciously violent as he explores his repressed masculine.

M. Esther Harding reveals something of this problem. On the one hand, she seems to praise the irrational, and on the other, she warns against it.

Mystical symbols of the feminine and masculine speak to us with enormous power: "Their strange nonrational logic will carry its own conviction and no rational proof of their truth will be necessary" (Harding 1971, 38; *see also* 81–82). Yet, in Harding's chapter on the virgin goddess, she warns against displacing conventionality with egocentricity when letting loose in the sensual realm. Genuine love must be safeguarded as a prime value.

It is easy to see how the lack of a clear distinction between negative and positive traits can lead to vagueness about ethical norms and the commitments involved. It is not uncommon to hear women involved in the imagery of wholeness justify experimental sexual activity, contraception, abortion, divorce, or leaving their children by saying that they are just not "ready" for the full commitment required to be a wife or a mother. But such decisions deeply wound the feminine.

Homosexuality, as a lifestyle as well as an orientation, is sometimes also justified as an opportunity to explore the feminine or masculine side of a personality. (Some books on healing of homosexuality by Nicolosi and Harvey, though mainly about male homosexuality, can be helpful for lesbian-oriented women—see "References" at the end of this book.)

Such ambiguity or deviance from Christian moral norms, even among religious people immersed in wholeness theory, reflects the tendency to make the individual and his processes into a sort of absolute, or idol, to which others may have to be sacrificed.

For instance, Jungian analyst Ann Ulanov, in *Receiving Woman,* describes new ways that women are seeking themselves. She writes:

> A woman in her fifties leaves her marriage of many years because she knows it to have been a pretense that damaged both parties and their children. She is not at all certain who she is or where she belongs. By seizing the outer truth she hopes to find her way to the inner one. Though criticized by her ex-husband as selfish in her action of divorce, she believes she gives a gift to him and to their children: an example, even if confused and groping, of trying to live out who one truly is. She finds this less painful and more life-giving than persisting in a false identity. (Ulanov 1981, 28)

A more drastic example is given in Doris Lessing's *Children of Violence* (1970). A girl brought up in a puritanical household becomes wild in her teens. Then she seeks security in a conventional marriage. But she finds being a mother to be stifling, in spite of the ample help of servants and other luxuries of her middle-class South African life. While her daughter is still a young child, she abruptly abandons her home to seek fulfillment through immersion in Communist activities.

Returning to Ann Ulanov's example, she does not claim that divorce is good in itself. This would not be the way a wholeness theorist would express herself. Instead, she leaves out the moral question entirely, and makes the individual's exploration of the destiny of self more important.

Giving such absolute value to the individual often accompanies a tendency to view the divine, not as a Trinity of really existing Persons, but rather as images that symbolize the nameless transcendent. Harding writes of the virginity of Mary as one of a number of instances of virgin goddess symbols. The factual validity of this doctrine is not proposed but rather is left vague.

Yet I maintain that such a lack of clarity about the objectivity of Divine Persons actually militates against the complete feminine experience that Jungians are so eager to foster. Trustful, peaceful surrender to the Divine Persons depends upon faith. Otherwise a certain non-directional inwardness in prayer and meditation contributes to negative feminine self-absorption.

A similar problem can arise in close relationships between women and men because of the idolization of the process. In a subtle manner people can view members of the opposite sex, not as unique, lovable personalities in themselves, but as stepping stones, as the means to fostering an individual's psychological processes. "He brings out the feminine in me; that's why I love him." "She brings out the masculine in me; that's why I love her." The language of projection can make it appear that the beloved has no independent qualities whatsoever: "You are projecting your inner masculine on that man." Is he just a blank screen ready to be projected on? Of course not, but the lack of a full metaphysics of the precious goodness of the person can impede the woman's grateful response to the real qualities of the other, depriving her of one part of the positive feminine experience of affirmation.

Others question whether targeting feminine or masculine qualities, such as nurturing or freedom, is the way to acquire them. Participating in many different kinds of human-potential workshops can create the illusion that one can arrive at wholeness through persistent experimentation and introspection. But desired traits often arise more naturally through our responding to the challenges of life—by focusing outside ourselves. For example, a woman who has never heard of methods for bringing out her femininity may realize it simply by carrying a baby to term. Her tender, empathetic characteristics will emerge in response to the baby rather than as a result of artificial methods. Similarly, a man or woman may develop leadership traits by accepting new responsibilities rather than by joining consciousness-raising groups.

The wholeness model fosters a somewhat misleading image of the strong woman who seeks her own salvation by means of a series of courageous interior adventures. This risk-taking sounds wonderful, particularly in contrast to the mindless way many of us are formed by a value-anemic culture. What is left out, however, is our ultimate vulnerable dependency on God and other loving persons for the discovery of the deepest meaning of our lives. How faith in God fulfills the dream of feminine and free will be the subject of the final section.

III. Faithful

6
Faithful Femininity

How can we acquire a wholly feminine spirit? In Christ. Through his grace, through faithfulness to him, we can arrive at inner wholeness and peace. In his love we can become truly feminine, strengthening the positive and diminishing the negative. Of course, coming to true femininity in all its purity and beauty can take a lifetime. But even the growing process can bring joy and peace.

Femininity Transfigured in Christ

"In him all things were made" (cf. Jn 1:3).

If I were raising a girl today, when the feminine is under attack, I would tell her from earliest childhood that God had planned her to be a female, and that this was a plan of love. "Male and female he created them" (Gen 1:27).

Just as Jesus said, God could count every hair on her head. He who "knit her together in her mother's womb" (cf. Ps 139:13) certainly formed her as a unique personality to be manifest in the feminine form, in a female body.

Whenever my little daughter would see a cute baby I would tell her that someday she might be a mother and that this would be a great gift from God.

When I would read to her about the women saints who were sisters and nuns, I would explain that they had sacrificed being wives and mothers to be brides of Christ and that this made them not unsexed, but spiritual mothers.

I would also tell her about the holy single women who expressed their motherly warmth and care in tending the needy and in performing corporal and spiritual works of mercy. Their feminine charm was not stifled; it blossomed because of their love for Christ.

When my daughter would begin menstruating I would read to her about the martyrs and the stigmatists. She would learn that her own minor, but perhaps painful, monthly bleeding was not only a way to participate in Christ's suffering on the cross but also a way to prepare for her motherhood in God's kingdom. I would witness to her how I offered up my own monthly pain and discomfort for others, for the kingdom.

When she would begin to show interest in boys, I would make explicit for her the meaning of sexual attraction and marriage.

> The LORD God said, "It is not good that the man should be alone; I will make him a helper fit for him." . . . So the LORD God caused a deep sleep to fall upon the man, and while he slept took one of his ribs and closed up its place with flesh; and the rib which the LORD God had taken from the man he made into a woman and brought her to the man. Then the man said, "This at last is bone of my bones and flesh of my flesh; she shall be called Woman, because she was taken out of Man." Therefore a man leaves his father and his mother and cleaves to his wife, and they become one flesh. (Gen 2:18, 21–24)

Using examples from the love expressed daily in my own marriage, I would show her how the grace of this sacrament overcomes dissension and hurt. I would explain why marriage is sacred and how Jesus reaffirmed this bond.

> And Pharisees came up to him and tested him by asking, "Is it lawful to divorce one's wife for any cause?" He answered, "Have you not read that he who made them from the beginning made them male and female, and said 'For this reason a man shall leave his father and mother and be joined to his wife, and the two shall become one'? . . . What therefore God has joined together let no man put asunder. . . . For your hardness of heart Moses allowed you to divorce your wives, but from the beginning it was not so." (Mt 19:3–5, 6, 8–9)

I would summarize for her, or let her read for herself when she was old enough, what John Paul II wrote in his book *Original Unity of Man and Woman* (1981) about the mystery of the attraction of man and woman for each other and the great difference between real love and lust (John Paul II 1981). I would have her read Dietrich von Hildebrand's beautiful book *Marriage* (1984).

I would explain to her about her own fertility and the sacredness of her time of creative openness and how evil it is to damage and pervert this sacred time by using contraceptives. I would use this analogy: sex is for love and reproduction, just as the church building is for prayer and for the Mass. It would be terrible if during the Consecration the priest brought together the bread and the wine and then proclaimed: "This is *not* my body, *not* my blood." So, too, how irreverent to bring together the sperm and the egg and yet introduce life-destructive elements between them to bring death instead of life. (For further discussion of Catholic teaching on this and other issues, see my book *Christian Ethics and Your Everyday Life* [1979]; it provides texts from Scripture and Tradition for many controversial issues.) Those convinced that for *serious* reasons they must postpone having a child can still use the nonfertile time to express their love.

If my daughter saw casual sex on TV or among her friends, I would tell her how it would violate her own feminine desire for real closeness and warmth to be seriously close to someone who does not cherish her enough to want her forever. I would point out to her that many engaged couples break up, showing their love was not meant for their whole lives as Christ wishes true love to be.

I would use such intrinsic arguments as a foundation for the practical ones about not wanting to become pregnant when there is no "nest" for the baby. How sad that the child who might look like the beloved should be dreaded rather than cherished. And what a demonic rebellion against God to try to undo nature as he made it by killing a child in the womb!

I would teach her to use her intuitive gifts to distinguish between attraction that comes from loneliness and the real self-donation of a marriage in Christ.

If friends of mine considered divorce I would explain to my daughter how tragic this was. In discussing cases in which the woman was primarily

the victim or the marriage was invalid, I would counsel my daughter not to lose courage, but to see how
that woman had been blessed: she had loved a man
deeply and perhaps borne children who could never
have been exactly those individuals except for that
particular union of genes.

I would teach her to admire those brave unwed
mothers who bear their children after repenting of a
love affair and to pray for women who abort their
babies, that they may find forgiveness in Christ.

I would urge her to remain at home with her
children when they are young, and later to engage
in part-time work outside the home if a supplementary income is needed or to develop her God-given
talents that are not used in mothering.

If my daughter objected that since Vatican II
many Catholics make up their own minds in conscience about ethical issues concerning their
womanhood, I would provide direct quotations such
as the following from the documents of Vatican II:

> Often he [man] . . . sets himself up as the
> absolute measure of all things. . . . Enlight-
> ened by divine revelation she [the Church]
> can offer a solution. (Flannery 1975, *The
> Church in the Modern World*, n. 12, p. 913)

> Deep within his conscience man discov-
> ers a law which he has not laid upon himself
> but which he must obey. Its voice, ever call-
> ing him to love and to do what is good and to
> avoid evil, tells him inwardly at the right mo-
> ment: do this, shun that. For man has in his
> heart a law inscribed by God. His dignity lies
> in observing this law, and by it he will be
> judged. His conscience is man's most secret

core, and his sanctuary. There he is alone with God whose voice echoes in his depths. By conscience, in a wonderful way, that law is made known which is fulfilled in the love of God and of one's neighbor. Through loyalty to conscience Christians are joined to other men in the search for truth and for the right solution to so many moral problems which arise both in the life of individuals and from social relationships. Hence, the more a correct conscience prevails, the more do persons and groups turn aside from blind choice and try to be guided by the objective standards of moral conduct. (Flannery 1975, *The Church in the Modern World*, n. 16, p. 916)

Today there is an inescapable duty to make ourselves the neighbor of every man, no matter who he is, and if we meet him, to come to his aid in a positive way, whether he is an aged person abandoned by all, a foreign worker despised without reason, a refugee, an illegitimate child wrongly suffering for a sin he did not commit, or a starving human being who awakens our conscience by calling to mind the words of Christ: "As you did it to one of the least of these my brethren, you did it to me" (Mt. 25:40).

The varieties of crime are numerous: all offenses against life itself, such as murder, genocide, abortion, euthanasia and wilful suicide; all violations of the integrity of the human person, such as mutilation, physical and mental torture, undue psychological pressures; all offenses against human dignity, such as subhuman living conditions, arbitrary imprisonment, deportation, slavery, prostitution, the selling of women and children, degrading working conditions where men are treated as mere tools for profit rather than free and responsible persons: all these and the like are criminal: they poison civilization; and they debase the perpetrators more than the victims and militate against the honor of the creator. (Flannery 1975, *The Church in the Modern World,* n. 27, p. 928)

The well-being of the individual person and of both human and Christian society is closely bound up with the healthy state of conjugal and family life. Hence Christians today are overjoyed, and so too are all who esteem conjugal and family life highly, to witness the various ways in which progress is being made in fostering those partnerships of love and in encouraging reverence for human life; there is progress too in services available to married people and parents for fulfilling their lofty calling: even greater benefits are to be expected and efforts are being made to bring them about.

However, this happy picture of the dignity of these partnerships is not reflected everywhere, but is overshadowed by polygamy, the plague of divorce, so-called free love and similar blemishes; furthermore, married love is too often dishonoured by selfishness, hedonism, and unlawful contraceptive practices. Besides, the economic, social, psychological, and civil climate of today has a severely disturbing effect on family life. . . .

The intimate partnership of life and the love which constitutes the married state has been established by the creator and endowed by him with its own proper laws: it is rooted in the contract of its partners, that is, in their irrevocable personal consent. It is an institution confirmed by the divine law and receiving its stability, even in the eyes of society, from the human act by which the partners mutually surrender themselves to each other; for the good of the partners, of the children, and of society this sacred bond no longer depends on human decision alone. For God himself is the author of marriage and has endowed it with various benefits and with various ends in view: all of these have a very important bearing on the continuation of the human race, on the personal development and eternal destiny of every member of the family, on the dignity, stability, peace, and prosperity of the family and of the whole human race. By its very nature the institution of marriage and married love is ordered to the procreation and education of the offspring and it is in them that it finds its crowning glory. Thus the man and woman, who "are no longer two but one" (Mt. 19:6), help and serve each other by their marriage partnership; they become conscious of their unity and experience it more deeply from day to day. The intimate union of marriage, as a mutual giving of two persons, and the good of the children demand total fidelity from the spouses and require an unbreakable unity between them. (Flannery 1975, *The Church in the Modern World,* nn. 47, 48; pp. 949, 950)

God, the Lord of life, has entrusted to men the noble mission of safeguarding life, and men must carry it out in a manner worthy of themselves. Life must be protected with the utmost care from the moment of conception: abortion and infanticide are abominable crimes. Man's sexuality and the faculty of reproduction wondrously surpass the endowments of lower forms of life; therefore the acts proper to married life are to be ordered according to authentic human dignity and must be honored with the greatest reverence. When it is a question of harmonizing married love with the responsible transmission of life, it is not enough to take only the good intention and the evaluation of motives into account; the objective criteria must be used, criteria drawn from the nature of the human person and human action, criteria which respect the total meaning of mutual self-giving and human procreation in the context of true love; all this is possible only if the virtue of married chastity is seriously practiced. In questions of birth regulation the sons of the Church, faithful to these principles, are forbidden to use methods disapproved of by the teaching authority of the Church in its interpretation of the divine law.

Let all be convinced that human life and its transmission are realities whose meaning is not limited by the horizons of this life only: their true evaluation and full meaning can only be understood in reference to man's eternal destiny. (Flannery 1975, *The Church in the Modern World*, n. 51, p. 955)

I would encourage her to read *Familiaris Consortio*, the "Apostolic Exhortation on the Family" (1981), for beautifully articulated affirmations of Church teaching on the family and also on the witness of virgins. In this document, as elsewhere, Pope John Paul II raises important points about social ethics. The feminine role of maternity must be supported by society. Women who would wish to be full-time mothers must not be forced to work outside the home. In accordance with this teaching I believe certain feminist positions concerning maternity and paternity leave, flexible time for mothers and fathers, equitable laws concerning credit, and so forth should be complemented by greater parish involvement in support services for women at all phases of their lives.

Let us turn to another topic concerning the feminine transfigured in Christ. My hypothetical daughter might be troubled about marriage and wonder how to make decisions in relation to her husband. I would help her reflect on these words of St. Paul and St. Peter:

> Be subject to one another out of reverence for Christ. Wives, be subject to your husbands, as to the Lord. For the husband is the head of the wife as Christ is the head of the church, his body, and is himself its Savior. As the church is subject to Christ, so let wives also be subject in everything to their husbands. Husbands, love your wives, as Christ loved the church and gave himself up for her, that he might sanctify her, having cleansed her by washing of water with the word. . . . Even so husbands should love their wives as their own bodies. He who loves his wife loves himself. . . .
>
> Let each one of you love his wife as himself, and let the wife see that she respects her husband. (Eph 5:21–26, 28, 33)

Likewise you wives, be submissive to your husbands, so that some, though they do not obey the word, may be won without a word by the behavior of their wives, when they see your reverent and chaste behavior. Let not yours be the outward adorning with braiding of hair, decoration of gold, and wearing of robes, but let it be the hidden person of the heart with the imperishable jewel of a gentle and quiet spirit, which in God's sight is very precious. . . . Let nothing terrify you.

Likewise, you husbands, live considerately with your wives, bestowing honor on the woman as the weaker sex, since you are joint heirs of the grace of life, in order that your prayers may not be hindered.

Finally, all of you, have unity of spirit, sympathy, love of the brethren, a tender heart and a humble mind. Do not return evil for evil or reviling for reviling; but on the contrary bless, for to this you have been called, that you may obtain a blessing. (1 Pet 3:1–4, 6–9)

Here I would warn her about extremes in male headship, yet have her ponder the views of St. Augustine, St. Thomas Aquinas, and of John Paul II.

Saint Augustine, in his *Confessions* (Book IX), described his mother, St. Monica, as subject to her husband through God. She spoke about God to her pagan husband as often as she could. When he exploded in anger she would calm him down and then give her side of the matter. For her own sake, to avoid his constant anger, she played the role of servant. Through her peaceful methods she eventually succeeded in bringing her husband to Christ. After his conversion, his character was reformed. In other words, by practicing submission as a positive feminine trait she was able to help her husband abandon his negative masculine traits and assume positive ones. The Christian man does rule his obedient wife; Christian headship is a service of love in duty and must never come out of love of power.

Although he accepted different roles for men and women, St. Augustine understood those passages which state that man and woman were made in the image of God as proof, beyond doubt, that women and men are equal in mind and soul (*Confessions,* Book XIII). Saint Thomas Aquinas followed St. Augustine in this matter. He thought women were equal to men in spiritual dignity but had weaker wills and hence were in need of male leadership. Is this why many women seek out male leadership—for ballast?

I would also refer her to John Paul II's *Mulieris Dignitatem,* from which some passages on male leadership you will find later in this chapter.

In general, I would want to witness to my daughter that it is worthwhile to "lay down one's life" for others in imitation of Christ. I would hope she would see from my own example that one does not need to be perfect to be a wife and mother. Nor need one be perfect to be a single woman for Christ or to be a consecrated religious—for Christ is all-forgiving, eager to erase the past and to give us fresh energies to bear the burden of our womanly roles.

By being close to Christ, in the sacraments and in prayer, we can fulfill our great feminine vocation: to live out our love for others day by day in faithfulness.

Finally, I would have my daughter steep herself in Marian devotion and frequently read the lives of women saints so that she could see how beautiful they were in their feminine warmth, charm, and faithfulness. (See my book *Treasury of Women Saints* [Ann Arbor: Servant, 1991].)

Mostly I would want my daughter and all women to study John Paul II's apostolic letter "On the Dignity and Vocation of Women" *(Mulieris Dignitatem).* It is a remarkable document. When I first read it, after working for so many years as a consultant to the United States bishops writing a pastoral on the concerns of women, I had tears in my eyes. We had struggled on our committee with so much anguish trying to make a clear statement about Catholic women's issues. Here was an answer coming from such a deep stratum of truth—written by a man, but with the greatest genuinely fatherly love for women, viewed as children of God, created with dignity, and called to an eternity of joy.

In this letter, the Holy Father insists that no matter how badly treated a woman may be, her essential dignity comes not from attitudes of weak and often sinful human beings, but from union with God. "This dignity consists *in the supernatural elevation to union with God*" (n. 4). Indeed, how many times have we faithful women of the Church found ourselves, after being beaten down by the world, kneeling in prayer before the Blessed Sacrament sensing gradually that, no matter what, we are beautiful in the eyes of God.

"For whenever man is responsible for offending a woman's personal dignity and vocation, he acts contrary to his own personal dignity and his own vocation" (n. 10).

While clearly condemning negative masculine attitudes and actions that have afflicted women of the past and do in the present, John Paul II wishes primarily to help women reflect on the goodness of the call to be loved by Christ, as illustrated by the example of his "style" in relating to women in Gospel times; of the call to family life, consecrated life, or of service and witness in society.

Aware of many sufferings of women in their maternal care, in the loneliness of widowhood, and in pangs of conscience caused by our own disordered decisions, he invokes the sorrowful Mother.

Most of all we are to grow in the vocation of love that comes from the sincere gift of self. It is in terms of this gift of self that the mutual subjection described in the Pauline Epistles is to be lived out. It is in terms of such a gift that we are to understand the sovereign right of Christ to choose to restrict his priestly call to men. Vocations are personal gifts, not rights.

The woman who knows Christ's sincere gift of himself to her in the uniqueness of her personal identity and the woman who gives herself to others in the overflow of this love is not likely to allow even deplorable injustices to rob her of her joy and hope.

Spiritual Healing of the Feminine

Most of us have been distorted to some extent in our own appropriation of our feminine natures. At various workshops I have suggested some paths for healing that seem to be effective:

1. Ponder in prayer the question of why God created you to be a woman.

2. Read the following passages from Scripture and see if they speak to you personally about the virtues mentioned:

gentleness: Prv 15:4; Jer 11:19; Mt 5:22; 11:29; Jn 8 (Christ's gentleness to the woman taken in adultery); Gal 5:22.

compassion: Dt 13:17; Ps 145:9; Is 40:1–2; 54:8; 66:12; Hos 11; Lk 7:13; 10:29 ff.; 15; 23:34; Col 3:12.

obedience: Ex 24:7; Is 1:19; Mt 26:39; Lk 2:15; 4; Rom 6; 1 Cor 14:34; Eph 5:22–33; 1 Tm 2:9–15; 2 Tm 4:1–5; Titus 2:5; 1 Pt 1:13–14; 3:1–7.

purity: Ps 24:3–4; 51; Mt 5:8, 28; Rom 1:26; Gal 5:19; Titus 2:5, 12; 1 Pet 3:1–7; Jude 7.

3. Return to the list of feminine traits that opened this chapter. Thank God for the positive ones you checked. Alone or with a prayer partner, look at your negative feminine traits and try to find their roots; then pray for healing of them. You could also pray to receive the positive traits you identified as ones you wish you had.

4. If you seek further healing in this area you might want to read my *Freed to Love: Healing for Catholic Women* (Sedona, Arizona: ChiaroOscuro Press, 1994). Videotapes of the teachings in this workshop are available from Franciscan University Press (1-800-783-6357).

7
Faithful Freedom

What is the source of true freedom for women? I believe the inspiration of the Holy Spirit is the source of true freedom together with obedience to him as he works through the Pope and the bishops in union with him.

We will consider some problems connected with patriarchy, language, and woman and roles in the Church. Finally, I will provide suggestions for spiritual healing for greater freedom.

Freedom Transfigured in Faith

Faith in a God of love who sacrificed himself for us to open the doors of heaven naturally leads to greater freedom. "The truth shall set you free."

Fear impedes spontaneity and daring, but perfect love casts out fear. The movement of the Holy Spirit in the heart of the believing woman should overcome passivity and strengthen leadership abilities. The objectivity of faith should replace subjective fancifulness and free the individual to interact fruitfully with reality.

Scripture inveighs against the negative male traits that have oppressed women. Men are told not to lord it over others (cf. 1 Pt 5:3). They should not be proud (cf. Rom 11:20; 2 Cor 10:5). Arrogance is blameworthy (cf. 1 Cor 4:18; 5:2; 2 Tm 3:2; Titus

1:7). Selfish ambitions are to be curbed (cf. 2 Cor 12:20; Gal 5:20). Other passages warn against being violent, lustful, shrewd, suspicious, and rash.

In Christ "there is neither Jew nor Greek . . . there is neither male nor female" (Gal 3:28). In Church teaching women have always been considered spiritually equal to men:

> All men [and women] are endowed with a rational soul and are created in God's image; they have the same nature and origin and, being redeemed by Christ, they enjoy the same divine calling and destiny; there is here a basic equality between all [human persons] and it must be given ever greater recognition.
>
> Undoubtedly not all [people] are alike as regards physical capacity and intellectual and moral powers. But forms of social or cultural discrimination in basic personal rights on the grounds of sex, race, color, social conditions, language or religion, must be curbed and eradicated as incompatible with God's design. It is regrettable that these basic personal rights are not yet being respected everywhere, as is the case with women who are denied the chance freely to choose a husband, or a state of life, or to have access to the same educational and cultural benefits as are available to men. (Flannery 1975, 929; *The Church in the Modern World,* 29)

The woman's strength in Christ begins at the very center of her desire to love and be loved:

> The deepest longing of woman's heart is to give herself lovingly, to belong to another, and to possess this other being completely. This longing is revealed in her outlook, per-

sonal and all-embracing, which appears to us as specifically feminine. But this surrender becomes a perverted self-abandon and a form of slavery when it is given to another person and not to God; at the same time, it is an unjustified demand which no human being can fulfill. Only God can welcome a person's total surrender in such a way that one does not lose one's soul in the process but wins it. And only God can bestow Himself upon a person so that He fulfills this being completely and loses nothing of Himself in so doing. That is why total surrender which is the principle of the [consecrated] religious life is simultaneously the only adequate fulfillment possible for woman's yearning. (Stein 1987, 52)

Although single and married women make this surrender in a different manner from their consecrated sisters, it is nonetheless true that Christ must be first before others, so that he has room to fill our deepest longings. We come to him each day in prayer and in the sacraments so that he can give himself to us. And his presence brings with it holy strength and true liberation.

The famous "Magnificat," which Mary sings in exultation about her role as mother of the Messiah, overflows with spontaneity, strength, and faith:

> My soul magnifies the Lord,
> and my spirit rejoices in God my Savior,
> for he has regarded the low estate
>   of his handmaiden.
> For behold, henceforth all generations
>   will call me blessed;
> for he who is mighty has done

> great things for me,
> and holy is his name. . . .
> He has scattered the proud
>   in the imagination of their hearts,
> he has put down the mighty
>   from their thrones,
> and exalted those of low degree;
> he has filled the hungry with good things,
> and the rich he has sent empty away.
>   (Lk 1:46–53)

The women saints are brave and bold, true leaders, devoted to the Faith; think of Joan of Arc and Catherine of Siena, for example. Even the "quieter" saints have been enormously influential because of the power of their spiritual courage—Jane Frances de Chantal, Thérèse of Lisieux, Elizabeth Ann Seton. No conventional roles for women in the society of their times could hold them back from fidelity to the inspirations of the Holy Spirit.

Mother Frances Cabrini, the first American citizen to be canonized, had a terror of the sea. Yet moved by the Spirit, she had the courage to take a ship from Italy to America to tend to the needs of her fellow immigrants, who were losing the Faith due to lack of the ministry of those who could speak Italian.

Many women mystics have written about their experiences of God. However, it was the combination of ecstasy with clarity of thought shown by Saints Catherine of Siena and Teresa of Avila that led to their being proclaimed doctors of the Church.

Blessed Anna Maria Taigi, wife of an Italian porter, loving mother of many children, instructed cardinals with the words the Lord sent her in prophecy.

What delights me in the lives of the women saints is their individuality. No two are alike. The strength of the Spirit within them freed them from rigid roles and the shackles of convention.

Once when trying desperately to figure out how to be assertive yet not aggressive, I realized that when I am truly in tune with the Holy Spirit, then I am sure I am doing the right thing, and I can fight for it valiantly without becoming threatening or abrasive. "God and I constitute a majority," as the humorous adage has it.

Grace perfects nature; it does not destroy it. The Spirit channels a woman's energies from manipulation, possessiveness, or seduction, into charming delicacy in love of neighbor, sincere openness in prayer, and surrender of beloved ones into the hands of God, who loves them more than she can.

When I am doing God's will in faith, I have peace, and peace strengthens me to be feminine and free. If we strive for the good rather than our own selfish aims, then a loving energy spills over from the feminine into the free, and from the free back into the feminine.

"We learn . . . to yield to a will that moves in us but is not our own, that does not snuff out our own will, but moves ours strongly into accord with its own" (Ulanov 1981, 26). Ann Ulanov views the experience of being a woman who is in touch with a larger reality, God, not as nullifying her personal identity, but as enlarging it.

It seems, however, that not all Christian women experience faith as lived in the Church as a source of freedom. Some Christian feminists claim that the use of masculinely oriented language makes women feel second class. Patriarchal structures denying leadership roles for women keep them in a subservient position.

On Inclusive Language

Any discussion of the issue of language must be preceded by a distinction between horizontal and vertical language. Horizontal language refers to other human beings such as "men and women," "brothers and sisters," "he and she." Vertical language concerns God or Persons of the Trinity.

Here is a small sample of Christian feminist viewpoints about language:

> The generic use of man as inclusive of woman does not always work, because too often when we hear *man* we understand male person not human person. . . . When we only refer to God as masculine, we render invisible that dimension of the divine best expressed by feminine images. (Riley 1985, 29)

Rosemary Reuther, in the article "Feminist Theology and Spirituality" in *Christian Feminism: Visions of a New Humanity* (San Francisco, 1984), proposes calling God "She/he" or the "God-ess."

Some want to see patriarchal words such as "Lord" and "Judge" eliminated in favor of "Creator" and "Source."

Since the first edition of *Feminine, Free, and Faithful,* there has been much more analysis of this difference. The bishops of the United States, in a document about liturgical use of biblical language (*Criteria for the Evaluation of Inclusive Language Translations,* NCCB, Nov. 15, 1990), hold that in many cases it is not only legitimate but helpful to translate horizontal language in an inclusive manner—that is, words for men or man can be translated as men and women or man and woman, where this was certainly the original intent of the biblical author. Care must be taken to avoid blanket re-translations so that masculine words which prophesy the Messiah to come or which reflect the presence of males only as in referring to the apostles, for example, are left unaltered.

The same document also forbids the use of feminine pronouns or nouns for God or for any of the three Persons of the Trinity.

This teaching stands against Christian feminist proposals that demand either equal use of feminine terms for Divine Persons or suggest constant substitution, say of Creator for Father. In his book *The Feminist Question,* Francis Martin explains that negative perceptions of the term Father coming from inordinate fear of earthly fathers or of God the Father need to be healed by meditation on the true positive meaning of fatherliness: generous, protective, caring.

Here are some other perspectives that you may wish to ponder concerning vertical language.

The desire to improve the status of women through making language about God more feminine may sound plausible on a strictly natural, rational level. But religions coming from Revelation are always supra-rational—that is, they start with God's initiative, not ours. For example, it is hard for us to understand only through reason why God would come to one particular group of people, the Jews, and form them to receive his truths in a special way. Why not send a special grace into the minds of all humans at the same time so that there would be just one religion worldwide? We don't really know why God didn't do it this way. But we do know that he didn't. As creatures, our task is not to correct God's "mistakes" but to ponder what he has revealed.

"The God of Abraham, Isaac and Jacob" is not the God of the philosophers. He reveals himself as Lord and Father and not only as "Creator-Source." He entered the world as a Son, not as a daughter or a unisex robot or a two-sexed, twin birth.

The best book I have read on this subject is by a Protestant theologian, Donald G. Bloesch. In *Battle for the Trinity: The Debate over Inclusive God Language* (1985) Bloesch argues that changes in symbolic images of God amount to rewriting the Bible to substitute a religion of experience. He makes startling comparisons with the way some German Christians during the Nazi period devised their own version of Christianity trying to "conserve what is abiding and reject what is stultifying. Their aim was to purge Christianity of its Jewish elements" (Bloesch, 70). Bloesch takes great exception to the gradual introduction of pagan symbols by some feminists. Here is a striking quotation from Ernst Bergmann, one of the German theologians identified by Bloesch: "I believe in the God of the German religion who is at work in nature, in the lofty human spirit, and in the strength of his people. I believe in the helper, Christ, who is struggling for the noble human soul" (Bloesch 1985, 70).

But isn't it true that there really are feminine aspects of God? Isn't he tender and nurturing?

A homey analogy might help in ordinary discussion with feminist thinkers. A son is talking to his mother. He says: "Mom, you know I think my Daddy is the sweetest, most loving father in the whole world." Dad overhears. He is pleased. Then the son adds: "I think I'll start calling him Mom from now on."

Why would Dad say No? Surely not because he thinks that only mothers should be loving and sweet, but because a father or dad is something ontologically different from a mother or mom.

On Leadership of Women in the Church

When considering leadership of women in the Church, it is important to distinguish between non-ordained pastoral ministry and the priesthood. The following illustrate the broad spectrum of feminist positions.

Many Christian women, whether they call themselves feminists or not, would like to see more women in pastoral, advisory, and decision-making roles in the Church. Verbal and, sometimes, monetary appreciation should accompany such ministry. In many geographical areas with a shortage of priests, women have assumed pastoral leadership.

Many Catholic feminists would like to see women also in ordained roles such as deacon and priest.

The May 2, 1985, *Origins* reported that "the New Testament evidence, while not decisive by itself, points toward the admission of women to priestly ministry" (from a report of the Catholic Biblical Association of America, 1979).

As renowned a theologian as Karl Rahner thought that there might be no sufficient evidence that the exclusion of women from the priesthood was a deliberate choice of Christ (see Karl Rahner, *Theological Investigations XX* [1981] and *In Memory of Her* by Elisabeth Schussler-Fiorenza [1984]).

Some male priests who have recommended ordination of women consider their exclusion to be an instance of extreme ethical injustice. They think women who leave the Roman Catholic Church in protest could be right.

Feminine base communities are often recommended as the center of Christian life for women, along with parallel participation in sexist institutional churches for revolutionary purposes (see *Christian Feminism: Visions of a New Humanity*, edited by Judith L. Weidman [1984]).

In the Roman Catholic Church a women's ordination conference in dialogue with the bishops is pressing for ordination as a right. Some women reportedly celebrating "Mass" already use feminist liturgies.

The Catholic Theological Society of America has researched the arguments for and against women's ordination (see the research report published by the Catholic Theological Society of America [1978]). Key points to consider are whether the exclusion of women from priesthood in the early Church was based on the will of Christ or rather on cultural conditions. Is it not possible that considerations of equality and need outweigh an outmoded tradition?

Some current findings seem to invalidate anthropological considerations based on theories of complementarity.

Can not a woman equally represent Christ since in Christ there is "neither male nor female"?

Regarding ordination of women, here are the main views given by the Vatican in its *Declaration on the Question of the Admission of Women to the Ministerial Priesthood* (1976, 8–11). For a thorough study of this issue, see Manfred Hauke's *Women in the Priesthood?* or a briefer work by Peter Kreeft and Alice von Hildebrand, *Women and the Priesthood* (1994).

Could the Church today depart from this attitude of Jesus and the apostles, which has been considered normative by the whole of tradition up to our own day? Various arguments have been put forward in favor of a positive reply to this question, and these must now be examined.

It has been claimed in particular that the attitude of Jesus and the apostles is explained by the influence of their milieu and their times. It is said that, if Jesus did not entrust to women and not even to his Mother a ministry assimilating them to the Twelve, it was because historical circumstances did not permit him to do so. No one, however, has ever proved—and it is clearly impossible to prove—that this attitude is inspired only by social and cultural reasons. As we have seen, an examination of the Gospels shows on the contrary that Jesus broke with the prejudices of the time, widely contravening the discriminations practiced toward women. One therefore cannot maintain that, by not calling women to enter the group of the apostles, Jesus was simply letting himself be guided by reasons of expediency. For all the more reason, social and cultural conditioning did not hold back the apostles from working in the Greek milieu, where the same forms of discrimination did not exist.

Another objection is based on the transitory character that some claim to see today in some of St. Paul's prescriptions concerning women, and upon the difficulties that some aspects of his teaching raise in this regard. But it must be noted that these ordinances, probably inspired by the customs of the period, concern scarcely more than disciplinary practices of minor importance, such as the obligation imposed on women to wear a veil on the head (1 Cor 11:2–16); such requirements no longer have a normative value. However, the Apostle's forbidding women "to speak" in the assemblies (see 1 Cor 14:34–35; 1 Tm 2:12) is of a different nature, and exegetes define its meaning in this way: Paul in no way opposes the right, which he elsewhere recognizes as possessed by women, to prophesy in the assembly (1 Cor 11:5); the prohibition solely concerns the official function of teaching in the Christian assembly. For St. Paul this prescription is bound up with the divine plan of creation (1 Cor 11:7; Gen 2:18–24): it would be difficult to see in it the expression of a cultural fact. Nor should we forget that St. Paul gave us one of the most vigorous texts in the New Testament on the fundamental equality of men and women, as children of God in Christ (see Gal 3:28). Therefore we have no reason to accuse him of prejudices against women when we note the trust he shows toward them and the collaboration he asks of them in his apostolate.

But over these objections taken from the history of apostolic times, those who support the legitimacy of change in the matter turn to the Church's practice in her sacramental discipline. It has been noted, in our day especially, to what extent the Church is conscious of possessing a certain power over the sacraments, even though they were instituted by Christ. She has used this power down through the centuries to determine their signs and the conditions of their administration: recent decisions by Popes Pius XII and Paul VI are proof of that. However, it must be emphasized that this power, which is a real one, has definite limits. As Pope Pius XII recalled: "The church has no power over the substance of the sacraments, that is to say, over what Christ the Lord, as the sources of Revelation bear witness, determined should be maintained in the sacramental sign." This was already the teaching of the Council of Trent, which declared: "In the Church there has always existed this power, that in the administration of the sacraments, provided that their substance remains unaltered, she can lay down or modify what she considers more fitting either for the benefit of those who receive them or for respect toward those same sacraments, according to varying circumstance, times, or places."

Moreover, it must not be forgotten that the sacramental signs are not conventional ones. Not only is it true that, in many respects, they are natural signs because they respond to the deep symbolism of actions and things, but they are more than that: they are principally meant to link the person of every period to the supreme Event of the history of salvation, to enable that person to understand, through all the Bible's wealth of pedagogy and symbolism, what grace they signify and produce. For example, the sacrament of the Eucharist is not only a fraternal meal, but at the same time the memorial that makes present and actual Christ's sacrifice and his offering by the Church. Again, the priestly ministry is not just a pastoral service; it ensures the continuity of the functions entrusted by Christ to the apostles and the continuity of the powers related to those functions. Adaptation of civilizations and times therefore cannot abolish, on essential points, the sacramental reference to constitutive events of Christianity and to Christ himself.

In the final analysis, it is the Church, through the voice of her Magisterium, that decides in these various domains what can change and what must remain immutable. When she judges that she cannot accept certain changes, it is because she knows she is bound by Christ's manner of acting. Her attitude, despite appearance, is therefore not one of archaism but of fidelity: it can be truly understood only in this light. The Church makes pronouncements in virtue of the Lord's promise and the presence of the Holy Spirit, to proclaim better the mystery of Christ and to safeguard and manifest the whole of its rich content.

This practice of the Church therefore has a normative character: in the fact of conferring priestly ordination only on men, it is a question of an unbroken tradition throughout the history of the Church, universal in the East and in the West, and alert to repress abuses immediately. This norm, based on Christ's example, has been and is still observed because it is considered to conform to God's plan for his Church.

In 1994 Pope John Paul II issued a formal statement regarding the debate concerning the ordination of women. The document, *On Reserving Priestly Ordination to Men Alone*, includes these words, regarded by many theologians as stated in an infallible manner:

> Wherefore, in order that all doubt may be removed regarding a matter of great importance, a matter which pertains to the Church's divine constitution itself, in virtue of my ministry of confirming the brethren (Luke 22:32) I declare that the Church has no authority whatsoever to confer priestly

ordination on women and that this judgment is to be definitively held by all the Church's faithful.

Still, many women influenced by feminist thinking wonder why. They may accept the teaching, but still be unsure why it must be so. I have found it helpful in discussions to offer the following perspectives.

Consider that it is dualistic to argue, as many Christian feminists do, that Jesus is primarily a person, not a male. The philosopher Mary F. Rousseau (1981) thinks that it is an essential part of human experience that others present themselves to us as male or female. To eliminate sexuality from the symbolic reenactment of the Sacrifice of the Cross in the Mass, the great nuptial act of the Bridegroom and the Bride, would have tremendously disruptive consequences. I agree. As a convert from philosophical atheism, one of the most exciting features of Christianity for me is that *truth* is a *person*, divine yet visualizable. Reality is a drama, not a syllogism.

I would find it as strange to have Christ played by a woman in the liturgical scenario as to have Mary played by a man in a nativity scene to indicate that men are parents too.

As to the cultural argument, we should realize that God formed the culture of this people. He could have formed an alternate culture with matriarchal structures and been incarnated as a woman and later represented by woman priests.

Sister Mary Neill, O.P., a theologian who considers herself a feminist, nonetheless supports the perennial teaching about non-ordination of women.

Reasoning from Jungian archetypal thinking, she says that since every human being receives his or her original nurturing food from the mother in the womb, it is necessary for us to receive our super-natural food "the Body and Blood of Christ" from the male side—from male priests representing Christ.

The Church's all-male priesthood does not exclude women from other roles of leadership, as is amply demonstrated in the history of the Church in her women witnesses, prophetesses, foundresses, doctors, teachers, and ministers to the ill and the poor.

The idea that Christian women cannot come into their own strengths as free women in Christ because of existing mindsets and patterns in the Church is certainly false; yet the concerns of feminism should not be dismissed as having no basis whatever.

It seems that becoming aware of feminine imagery of God in Scripture, while not proving that God is revealed equally as feminine and masculine, does help us to get in touch with this dimension, and is especially helpful for Christians who overemphasize God as power.

I would welcome more education for Church men, religious and lay, on the problem of oppressive, negative masculine traits such as cold, arrogant, smug, and domineering behavior. Chronic problems of brutality and sexual abuse, where they occur, must be addressed more forcefully.

On the other hand, as explained above, too many errors in theory and practice are connected with most Christian feminist ideas for anyone to embrace this movement as essentially positive. Besides the tendency to replace biblical revelation and Church authority with subjective ideas, there is also a growing tendency to accept abortion in many cases under the deceptive title of "reproductive freedom." On this and many other moral questions, only a small percentage of women calling themselves Christian feminists accept Church teaching without dissent.

This does not mean that all those who identify with feminism hold all these false concepts. It is important for women who stand against feminism as a whole to be sensitive to those Christian feminists who are strongly pro-life and who do accept Church teaching and practice.

I believe that the crucial difference between feminists is whether one has enough faith in Christ's promises that it is possible to accept suffering for the kingdom in ways that touch our hope for personal happiness. When we experience the personal love of God for us, it is easier to see how intertwined are femininity, freedom, and faithfulness.

Mary, Our Mother

For the Christian woman, the most beautiful image of womanhood—feminine, free, and faithful—will always be Mary, the Mother of God. Created perfectly without sin by God the Father, indwelt by the Holy Spirit, and filled by Christ, the Son, she is the dove, the feminine handmaid, and the fire of the Magnificat.

Think of the courage of a woman ready to be stoned to death by her people in obedience to a message that could only have sounded insane to any person she might confide it to! Think of her trust in the midst of anguish, hearing that innocents would be put to death and women convulsed in misery as Herod sought her Son and gave the brutal command to murder all the young male babies of the region of Bethlehem. Think of her deep delight in sharing in the secrets of her Son's future mission, later telling of his hidden life, strengthening the apostles who would be going to martyrdom!

The dogmas about Mary, unfortunately too often symbolized in saccharine statues, are nonetheless strong in their imagery. She is the woman who will crush the serpent under her heel, for she is the Immaculate Conception. She was assumed into heaven where she continues to minister to the Church, to intercede for us, to come to us in apparitions as Bride of God and Mother of the people of God, so unsentimental as to demand of a soft generation the rigors of fasting and penance. Mother Mary pleads for the life of her children. Cardinal Ratzinger writes in his book *Daughter Zion:* "Woman . . . is the mother of all life. . . . In this way the undestroyed dignity and majesty of woman are expressed. She preserves the mystery of life, the power opposed to death; for death is like the power of nothingness, the antithesis of Yahweh, who is the creator of life and the God of the living" (Ratzinger 1983, 17).

Mary is an icon of all the positive feminine traits: receptivity, delicacy, warmth, empathy, purity, beauty. Yet she is also as strong, as wise, as true, as courageous, as any male saint.

In going through my notes for a book I wrote with Sister Mary Neill, O.P., *Bringing the Mother with You: Healing Meditations on the Mysteries of Mary,* I came upon a meditation I had made at that time. It still seems beautiful and so I insert it here:

> In every woman there is the longing to be
> Mary—a pure flame of the sun. A woman who
> is a bonfire can enkindle—Yes!—but cannot

give sustained warmth and light to her children.

Joseph holds the Mary in us still, that we may know God, make our assent to be the Christ-bearer. He protects his bride, builds the house around her, the Church, so that the onrushing evil forces should not prevail while New Life is being born. When the Josephs become Judases, the Marys become Eves cast out of Eden, buried in Sheol.

O Lord Jesus, unwind the shroud and resurrect your Church. Our Lady of Guadalupe, sublime stillness of the sun, intense enough to char your impress through our human cloaks, intercede for us.

And I hear Mary answering that prayer of mine, for she is the promise of our own celestial joy when we shall be feminine and free in the eternal kingdom—in the words of Zephaniah:

> Sing aloud, O daughter of Zion;
> shout, O Israel!
> The LORD your God is in your midst. . .
> he will rejoice over you with gladness,
> he will renew you in his love;
> he will exult over you with loud singing
> as on a day of festival. (Zeph 3:14, 17, 18)

Spiritual Healing for Greater Freedom

Here are some ways you might choose to make the ideas in this chapter on freedom more personal to you:

1. Ask yourself when you have felt most free as a woman.

2. Read some of these Scriptures about aspects of freedom and ponder their message:

courageous: Jos 1:9; 1 Chr 19:13; Ps 27; Lam 1:6; Jn 11:16; 2 Cor 6:4–10. Making the Stations of the Cross can give us courage as we realize how much Jesus suffered.

leading: Meditating on the lives of David, the prophets, and Christ, we can see how they take the lead rather than follow societal patterns.

strong: 1 Kgs 2:1–2; Ps 24:8; 136:12; Prv 23:11; Song 8:6; 1 Is 35:3–4; Lk 1:80; Rom 4:20; Eph 6:10–20.

just: Dt 33:21; Ps 111:1–8; Ps 145:17; Prv 12:5; Is 11:1–5; 61:8; Mt 1:19; Jn 5:30; Phil 4:8.

self-controlled: Prv 25:28; 1 Cor 7:5; 9:25; Gal 5:16–25; 2 Tm 1:7; Titus 1:8; 2 Pet 1:6.

3. Go through the list of traits associated with freedom. Thank God for those positive ones you checked. Look at any negative ones that are yours and pray for healing of these as you explore their roots.

4. Have you ever been oppressed by rigidity in feminine roles or by masculine rejection of your equality? If so, can you forgive those who have hurt you? Pray for greater freedom and strength of character.

5. If you have sinned because of selfishness in pursuing your own fulfillment, you can repent and receive Christ's forgiveness in prayer and confession.

6. Meditate on the lives of Mary and other women saints for inspiration and intercession.

Since the publication of the first edition of *Feminine, Free, and Faithful,* I have started giving workshops entitled "Freed to Love: Healing for Catholic Women." You can obtain a booklet with the workshop talks and prayers as well as instructions for bringing these sessions to local areas by calling ChiaroOscuro Press, 1-800-437-2368. Videos of me giving the teachings are available from Franciscan University Press, 1-800-783-6357.

8

A Creed for Christian Women

I believe that God, the Father, created me
  a *person: human, spiritual, immortal*
      —not a doll
      —not a sex object
      —not a slave
  a *feminine person*
      —because God thought that my unique soul
        could best express itself as feminine
  with a *beautiful feminine body*
      —to be clothed according to its shape
      —to be joined in overflowing eternal love to
        my spouse

      or

      —to be consecrated to himself in the mystical
        adventure of celibacy

      or

      —to remain hidden in him, if he wills,
        suspended in the world an unvowed free
        presence to all
  capable of the *sacred act of transmitting his life
  to creatures,* and therefore
      —not to be sold for gain
      —not to be bartered for passing pleasure,
        popularity, or security
      —not to be nullified in creativity by
        contraceptive devices

—not to allow the killing of my own fruit
—but instead to be open to the life-giving seed
  of my husband
  bring forth new life
  hold my babies close
  feed them from my substance

I believe that God, the Son, as Jesus the Christ
  redeemed the image of God broken in me by my
  destructive conditioning of
  —family
  —school
  —the world at large
  —the weight of our history
comes to heal me with the same absolute love he
gave to my ancient sisters
  —Mary
    announcing his love for me in his
    baptismal kiss
  —Martha
    in daily familiar yet holy communion
  —Mary Magdalene
    in Penance's purging love embrace
teaches me *the path of sacrificial love,* never to
seek
  —self-fulfillment at the expense of the growth
    of my sisters and brothers
  —friendships of convenience
  —the destruction of unwanted babies
  —first place over husband and children
  —first place over others at work
always to show loving kindness to others, and
even to myself, even when we are
  —boxed-in, not "open"
  —weak, not "strong"
  —needy, not "beautiful"

inspires me to hope for
- —understanding, emerging even out of friction
- —reconciliation not divorce
- —renewal not disaster

by the influx of his surprising, fresh,
unpredictable, infinite flow of grace

I believe in God, the Holy Spirit
kindling the first flame of
- —my God-given talents
- —hidden crazy dreams
- —my unending search for beauty
- —my unquenchable longings for love

fanning the flame of my desire for being by
- —the stunning loveliness of nature
- —the fleeting promise of bliss in human love
- —the sudden sweetness of small acts
- —the amazing, forgiving, stable love of others
  for me
- —the haunting inspiration of the bold and
  holy saints

raking the coals to recover the flame buried under
- —limited images others had and have of me
- —the put-downs of teachers and companions
- —my own fear, apathy, failure, and despair

that You and I and We might form *communities
of growth and love*
- —at home
- —at work
- —in the world around

in spite of all our faults
on earth as it is in heaven

I believe in the mystical body of the Church because
in spite of
- —our sins

—our ignorance
—our misery

we have preserved the vision of the immortal infinite equality of all people female and male before God

we have taught the seeking not of his will or her will but of God's will

we have known Christ's love pouring through us not as me and you or she and he but as One Body

we have faith in him and proof in him that not degradation, frustration, hate, or despair, but *love* will have the victory in the eternal kingdom.

And in her, our Holy Church, I embrace my sisters
  —longing, straining, seeking ones, and
    frustrated, miserable, despairing ones who
    yet hope in God
  —patient, holy martyrs of motherhood and
    irritable unhappy ones whom God blesses
    and forgives
  —mystical, celibate souls on fire with celestial
    love and empty, saddened ones whom God
    will one day fill to overflowing

together enfolded in the ample, azure mantle of
  Our Lady of Liberation
  Virgin, Mother, Saint

who accomplished the impossible
  by total openness to God

Alleluia, Amen!

References

Abeel, Erica. "The Love and Rape of Jean Harris." *Savvy* (April 1981).

Allen, Prudence. *The Concept of Woman*. Montreal: Eden Press, 1985.

Andelin, Helen. *Fascinating Womanhood*. New York: Bantam, 1990.

Bardwick, Judith. *In Transition: How Feminism, Sexual Liberation, and the Search for Self-fulfillment Have Altered America*. New York: Holt, Rinehart and Winston, 1979.

Bloesch, Donald G. *Battle for the Trinity: The Debate over Inclusive God Language*. Ann Arbor, Mich.: Servant, 1985.

Blumenfeld, Samuel. *The Retreat from Motherhood*. New Rochelle, N.Y.: Arlington House, 1975.

Bouyer, Louis. *Woman in the Church*. Trans. Marilyn Teichert. San Francisco: Ignatius Press, 1979.

Caprio, Betsy. *The Woman in the Tower*. New York: Paulist Press, 1983.

Catholic Theological Society of America. Research report on women's ordination. Manhattan College, Bronx, NY 10471.

Chervin, Ronda. *Living in Love: About Christian Ethics*. Boston: St. Paul Books and Media, 1988.

————, and Sr. Mary Neill. *Bringing the Mother with You: Healing Meditations on the Mysteries of Mary.* New York: Seabury, 1982.

————. *The Woman's Tale.* New York: Seabury, 1980.

————, and Terri Vorndran Nichols. *Woman to Woman.* San Francisco: Ignatius Press, 1988.

————. *Treasury of Women Saints.* Ann Arbor: Servant, 1991.

————. *Prayers of the Women Mystics.* Ann Arbor: Servant, 1992.

————. *Freed to Love: Healing for Catholic Women.* Sedona, Ariz.: ChiaroOscuro, 1994.

Chesterton, G. K. *What's Wrong with the World?* 1942.

Cross, Nancy. *Christian Feminism.* Front Royal, Va.: Christendom Publications, 1984.

de Beauvoir, Simone. *The Second Sex.* Translated and edited by H. M. Parshley. New York: Alfred A. Knopf, 1952.

Declaration on the Question of the Admission of Women to the Ministerial Priesthood. Washington, D.C.: United States Catholic Conference, 1976.

Durden-Smith, Jo. "Male and Female—Why?" *The Collegiate Career Woman* (Winter), 1980.

The Feminist Papers. Edited by Alice S. Rossi. New York: Columbia University Press, 1973.

Flannery, Austin. *Vatican Council II. The Conciliar and Postconciliar Documents.* Northport, N.Y.: Costello Publishing Co., 1975.

Friedan, Betty. *The Feminine Mystique.* New York: Dell Books, 1971. (First published in 1963. New York: Norton).

Gilligan, Carol. *In a Different Voice.* Cambridge: Harvard University Press, 1982.

Greer, Germaine. *The Female Eunuch.* New York: Bantam, 1972.

Harding, M. Esther. *Woman's Mysteries.* New York: Harper Colophon, 1971. For a fascinating description of negative and positive ways of relating to the psychological impact of the menstrual cycle, see 64–83.

Hauke, Manfred. *Women in the Priesthood?* Translated by David Kipp. San Francisco: Ignatius, 1986.

Harvey, John. *The Homosexual Person.* San Francisco: Ignatius Press.

Hilberman, Elaine, M.D. Overview: The "Wife Beater's Wife" reconsidered. *The American Journal of Psychiatry* 1337 (November 1980): II.

John Paul II. *Familiaris Consortio.* Boston: Daughters of St. Paul, 1981.

———. *Original Unity of Man and Woman.* Boston: Daughters of St. Paul, 1981.

———. *Mulieris Dignitatem* (On the Dignity and Vocation of Women). Boston: St. Paul Books and Media, 1988.

———. *On Reserving Priestly Ordination to Men Alone.* Boston: St. Paul Books and Media, 1994.

Jones, E. Michael. The Asymmetry of the Sexes. *Affirmations,* 1984.

Kippley, John and Sheila. *The Art of Natural Family Planning.* Lewiston, N.Y.: Life Cycle Books.

Lessing, Doris. *Children of Violence.* New York: New American Library, 1970.

Lorde, Audre. *The Black Unicorn.* New York: W. W. Norton & Co, 1978.

Mahowald, Mary B. *Philosophy of Women.* Indianapolis: Hackett Publishing Co., 1978. References to Mahowald excerpts apply to these works: Atkinson, Ti-Grace. "Radical Feminism." In *Amazon Odyssey;* Aristotle. "On the Generation of Animals." In *Generation of Animals.* Trans. by A. Peck; Engels, Frederich. "Origin of the Family." In *Origin of the Family, Private Property and the State;* Lenin, V. I. "The Woman Question." In *The Emancipation of Women;* Mill, John Stuart. "The Subjection of Women." In *On liberty;* Nietzsche, Friederich. "Of Womenkind, Old and Young. Of Child and Marriage." In *Thus Spake Zarathustra;* Russell, Bertrand. "The Liberation of Women." In *Marriage and Morals;* Wollstonecraft, Mary. *A Vindication of the Rights of Women;* Vilar, Esther. "What Is Woman?" In *The Manipulated Man.*

Marshner, Connie. *Can Motherhood Survive?* Brentwood, Tenn.: Wolgemuth and Hyatt Publishers, Inc., 1990.

Martin, Francis. *The Feminist Question.* Grand Rapids, Mich.: Wm. Eerdmans, 1994.

Masculine/Feminine. Edited by Betty and Theodore Roszak. New York: Harper Colophon Books, 1969.

Morgan, Marabel. *The Total Woman.* Old Tappan, N.J.: Fleming H. Revell, 1975.

Neill, Mary, Don Briel, and Ronda Chervin. *How Shall We Find the Father?* New York: Seabury, 1983.

Plato. Dialogues. All editions of Plato's dialogues are numbered in sections in the same way. Relevant sections follow: *Symposium* 190-193; *Timaeus* 41d-42a, b, c; *Republic* 454e, 455d; *Laws* 802e, 721-722.

Pro-Life Feminism. Edited by Gail Grenier-Sweet. Lewiston, N.Y.: Life Cycle Books.

Rahner, Karl. *Theological Investigations,* vol. 20. New York: Crossroad, 1981.

Ratzinger, Cardinal. *Daughter Zion.* Trans. John McDermott. San Francisco: Ignatius Press, 1983.

Riley, Maria. *In God's Image.* Kansas City, Mo.: Leaven Press, 1985.

Rousseau, Mary F. Theological trends: The Ordination of Women: A Philosopher's Viewpoint. *The Way* 21 (July 1981).

Sartre, Jean-Paul. *No Exit and Three Other Plays.* Trans. by L. Abel. New York: Vintage Books, 1949.

———. *Being and Nothingness.* Trans. by H. E. Barnes. London: McThuen, 1957.

Sayers, Dorothy. *Gaudy Night.* New York: Harper and Row, 1960.

Schussler-Fiorenza, Elisabeth. *In Memory of Her.* New York: Crossroad, 1984.

Stein, Edith. *Woman.* Translated by Freda Mary Oben. Washington, D.C.: ICS Publications, 1987.

Stern, Karl. *The Flight from Woman.* New York: Farrar, Straus and Giroux, 1965.

Tiger, Lionel and Robin Fox. *The Imperial Animal.* New York: Holt, Rinehart and Winston, 1971.

Ulanov, Ann Belford. *Receiving Woman.* Philadelphia: The Westminster Press, 1971.

Vilar, Esther. *The Manipulated Man.* New York: Farrar, Straus and Giroux, 1972. See especially 13-21.

von Balthasar, Hans Urs. Ephesians 5:21-33 and *Humanae Vitae:* A Meditation. *Christian Married Love.* Edited by Raymond Dennehy. San Francisco: Ignatius Press, 1981.

von Hildebrand, Alice. *By Grief Refined.* Steubenville, Oh.: Franciscan University Press, 1994.

――――. *By Love Refined.* Manchester, N.H.: Sophia Institute Press.

――――, and Peter Kreeft. *Women and the Priesthood.* Steubenville, Oh.: Franciscan University Press, 1994.

von Hildebrand, Dietrich. *Marriage.* Manchester, N.H.: Sophia Institute Press, 1984.

―――― and Alice. *Man and Woman.* Manchester, N.H.: Sophia Institute Press.

von Le Fort, Gertrud. *The Eternal Woman.* Translated by Placid Jordan. Milwaukee: Bruce Publishing Co., 1962.

Christian Feminism. Edited by Judith L. Weidman. San Francisco: Harper and Row, 1984.

Wojtyla, Karol. *Love and Responsibility.* Translated by H. T. Willets. New York: Farrar, Straus and Giroux, 1981.

Women's Liberation, Notes from the Third Year, an Annual. Edited by Anne Koedt and Shulamith Firestone. New York.

Freed to Love

A Healing Seminar for Catholic Women

by Ronda Chervin

Available from Franciscan University Press

To order call toll free: **1-800-783-6357**

Visa and MasterCard accepted

Other Books by Ronda Chervin

Available from Franciscan University Press

Freed to Love: Healing for Catholic Women
Six chapters of witness, teaching, healing prayer, and ideas for workshops and retreats.
OP186 .... $6.95

Prayers of the Women Mystics
Sketches of and prayers by women mystics: Teresa of Avila, Hildegard of Bingen, Margaret Mary Alacoque, Raissa Maritain, and more.
OP191 .... $8.99

A Mother's Treasury of Prayers
Old and new prayers for mothers of babies, children, teens, adults, and grandchildren.
OP190 .... $8.99

Signs of Love: About the Sacraments
Engaging booklet explaining the sacraments as signs of Christ's intimate love for us.
OP195 .... $1.95

Living in Love: About Christian Ethics
An explanation of Catholic moral teaching. Ideal for high school, college, RCIA, and adult catechesis.
OP193 .... $6.95

Treasury of Women Saints
Lives of 200 women saints—mothers, penitents, prophets, contemplatives—with applications for women today.
OP206 .... $12.99

Great Saints, Great Friends
For journal work, group sharing, and personal inspiration.
OP199 .... $7.95

Spiritual Friendship: Darkness and the Light
A good choice for those who struggle with compelling but unbalanced attachments or who want to learn how to love friends in a truly Christian way.
OP194.................. $8.95

Tell Me Why: Answers to Tough Questions about the Catholic Faith
Answers to questions of ex-Catholics, Protestants, atheists, and Jews.
OP189.................. $8.95

Voyage to Insight: Discovering Your Personal Philosophy of Life
Help open your non-Catholic friends to choices between non-religious and Christian world views and lifestyles.
OP196.................. $12.95

En Route to Eternity
Ronda Chervin, widow, mother, grandmother; convert to the Catholic faith from an atheistic Jewish background. Her life story.
OP192.................. $11.95

Quotable Saints
Wisdom of the saints arranged by topic for help in anxiety, doubt, etc.
OP203.................. $9.99

The Kiss from the Cross: A Saint for Every Kind of Suffering
From anguish to temptation, doubt to despair, showing how the saints made it through the worst trials we bear.
OP198.................. $9.99

A Treasury of Catholic Customs and Traditions
A handy guide to seasonal and daily customs.
OP202.................. $8.99

To order call toll free: **1-800-783-6357**
Visa and MasterCard accepted